Fifty Shades of Feminism

Edited by Lisa Appignanesi, Rachel Holmes & Susie Orbach

virago

VIRAGO

First published in Great Britain in 2013 by Virago Press

Introduction copyright © Lisa Appignanesi, Rachel Holmes
and Susie Orbach 2013

Pages 323–4 constitutes an extension of this copyright page.

The moral rights of the authors have been asserted.

A CIP catalogue record for this book
is available from the British Library.

ISBN 978-1-84408-945-1

Typeset in Bembo by M Rules
Printed and bound in Great Britain by
Clays Ltd, St Ives plc

Papers used by Virago are from well-managed forests
and other responsible sources.

MIX
Paper from
responsible sources
FSC® C104740

Virago Press
An imprint of
Little, Brown Book Group
100 Victoria Embankment
London EC4Y 0DY

An Hachette UK Company
www.hachette.co.uk

www.virago.co.uk

'Every time we liberate a woman,
we liberate a man'

Margaret Mead

'As a woman I have no country.
As a woman my country is the whole world'

Virginia Woolf

CONTENTS

Line drawings throughout by Posy Simmonds

FROM THE EDITORS

So there we were catching up, rectifying the state of the world and moaning, as friends do when they get together. We started talking about the wave of essentialism once more sweeping the woman's world. The phenomenon of *Fifty Shades of Grey* came up and Lisa suddenly said, 'What I'd really like to see is *Fifty Shades of Feminism*.' And the idea for this volume was born.

Of course, born is not made. Faster than the idea was conceived we began to tell ourselves and each other that as over-busy women we didn't have time to do it. But the necessity to do this book was compelling – the conversation, the connection between us and those we could bring together made us realize that, in fact, we didn't have any time left not to do it. Good ideas must be put into action.

With a wish list of talented contributors from all three of us, our initial fifty was soon nearer five hundred. And being a triumvirate of women relaxed with flexible figures we happily expanded our waistlines to accommodate the treats of poetry, cartoons and the fruits of Virago's competition to find out what feminism means to the under-twenty-fives. As we continued talking about what the great, recently departed Adrienne Rich called the potentially planet-transforming connections between women, we realized we would soon be at five thousand – even without all our favourite inspirational columnists who lead the way in regularly speaking their and our thoughts. Calling the final complement of fifty feminist shades for this volume was a great deal harder than picking a supermodel line-up. Unlike pre-fab images of commodified, categorized stereotypes of zip-lipped silent beauty, all our women come with distinct voices and ideas. There was no airbrushing of brain or size here.

Choosing just fifty women was difficult, but we soon realized that *Fifty Shades of Feminism* is a model that can be taken up and replicated by hundreds and thousands around the world. We'd like to think of this as a call to readers: use this as a new kind of supermodel and go out and find your own fifty. Every community can have its own feminist shades, connecting together into a world of conversations about where we are with feminism today.

After all, fifty years after the publication of Betty Friedan's pioneering *The Feminine Mystique*, have we as women really exchanged supposed purity and maternity to become vacuous desiring machines inspired only by variations of sex, shopping and masochism – all tinted luminescent neuro-pink to peddle the same old worn-out shades of miserable grey submissiveness?

We think not. In this volume, fifty women reflect on the shades that inspire them and what being a woman means to them and those around them today. There's no one kind of feminism and no one kind of feminist. And none of us in this collection has got time or life to spare to be cudgelling ourselves or other women with punitive –ists or –isms. This concert of shades is a multi-vocal chorus; it's often out of harmony, but it's carrying a tune and that tune is catching.

We're very pleased that this small volume contains women of all ages, with a rich mix of experience and expertise, world-class talents, spectacular frustrations and failures, knowledge, wit, wisdom, irony and passion. From a young barrister to a composer, to a gang-worker, to comedians, politicians, campaigners, academics, a psychoanalyst, poets, writers, theatre directors, actors, fighters, journalists, mothers, sisters, Dames and daughters, these are women who think, who do, and who inspire. They don't pretend to be representative and nor does this volume. Luckily, there are more than fifty walks of life and more than fifty types of women.

But these are brilliant ones. They made us laugh. They made us cry. They opened our eyes to different ways of seeing and being and thinking. They made us consider the meanings of feminism today and what remains to be done to make our condition, which is also the human condition, a better one. We hope they'll do the same for you.

Lisa Appignanesi, Rachel Holmes, Susie Orbach
March 2013

'If there's a book you really
want to read, but it hasn't been written
yet, then you must write it'

Toni Morrison

Margaret Atwood

'Update on Werewolves'

In the old days, all werewolves were male.
They burst through their bluejean clothing
as well as their own split skins,
exposed themselves in parks,
howled at the moonshine.
Those things frat boys do.

Went too far with the pigtail yanking –
growled down into the pink and wriggling
females, who cried Wee wee
wee all the way to the bone.
Heck, it was only flirting,
plus a canid sense of fun:
See Jane run!

But now it's different.
Now it's a global threat.
Long-legged women sprint through ravines
in furry warm-ups, a pack of kinky

models in sado French Vogue getups
and airbrushed short-term memories,
bent on no-penalties rampage.

Look at their red-rimmed paws!
Look at their gnashing eyeballs!
Look at the backlit gauze
of their full-moon subversive haloes!
Hairy all over, this belle dame,
and it's not a sweater.

O freedom, freedom and power!
they sing as they lope over bridges,
bums to the wind, ripping out throats
on footpaths, pissing off brokers.

Tomorrow they'll be back
in their middle-management black
and Jimmy Choos
with hours they can't account for
and first dates' blood on the stairs.
They'll make some calls: Goodbye.
It isn't you. I can't say why.
They'll dream of sprouting tails
at sales meetings,
right in the audiovisuals.
They'll have addictive hangovers
and ruined nails.

Notes on 'Update on Werewolves':

1. I was frightened as a child by Abbott and Costello films, and also
    by Quebec folktales about the Loup Garou.

2. After which I wrote a poem – in 1986 – called 'Werewolf Movies'.
3. In those days, all werewolves were men. As in *An American Werewolf in Paris*.
4. But now they aren't. Angela Carter has a wolvish female. There are female werewolf novels, and female werewolves in the Twilight series. So this poem is an update on the earlier poem.

'Update on Werewolves' first appeared in 2012 on Wattpad (www.wattpad.com).

I

Naomi Alderman

Wild West Video

I write novels, and I write video games.

I suppose it might seem obvious where I'd have the greater problem with sexism. After all, novels are a nice, safe, female-dominated industry with special prizes, magazines and imprints just for women. And video games? They're the Wild West. Lawless, aggressive, male-orientated. No place for a lady.

And it's true, games are sexist. Games conferences routinely employ 'booth babes' – scantily clad women to attract attention to their booths. Women in games are occasionally foxy large-breasted heroines and more often wordless love interest or dead-girlfriends-in-fridges put there solely to advance the male hero's plot. When games try to attract women players, they often do so by being amazingly 1960s-style patronizing. Want to appeal to girls? Surely you need games about fashion, make-up and ponies! Yes, it might seem obvious that the world of novels would be a haven for a woman writer, while the world of video games would be forbidding and unpleasant.

And yet. And yet.

Novels are, as they say, a well-developed market. They have their ways of doing things. Men, it's well known, don't buy novels written by women. Having decided early on not to call myself N. A. Alderman, I have to have girly jackets featuring women gazing wistfully at summer meadows. Even when the novel in question is mostly concerned with a relationship between two gay men. No point having a gender-neutral cover: men don't buy books written by women. Newspapers too, the statistics tell us, review fewer novels by women. Novels by women are less likely to be called 'important', women writers less likely to be thought of as essential voices. When each novel comes out, my kind publishers set me up to write pieces for women's magazines – this too is a well-developed market – about my personal experiences. 'What would you get me to do,' I ask, 'if I were a man?' If they know, they don't tell me; they can't make it happen. I'm a woman, writing. Therefore I'm a women's writer.

It's not like this in games. Because games are still largely male. Because there aren't yet large-scale 'games for women'. Because there's therefore no silo to put me in. It's more like, I imagine, a 1970s feminist storming a boardroom. Once you're in the boys' club, you're in, and there's no special girls' holding pen to put you in – they haven't invented one yet. No one's ever told me that my games have to be marketed a particular way because I'm a woman. No one's ever suggested I'd be better working on 'girls' games'. No one's ever asked me questions about my games that made me suspect they wouldn't ask that question of a man. I've had my authority and expertise questioned, sure. I've been mistaken for an assistant. That's OK. I know how to deal with that. And once I'm in, I'm in. One of the boys, talking about games, writing games. I get to put my head above the water, and breathe in deeply: yes, I'm here, I've broken through, now I get judged according to the same criteria as everyone else.

So which is worse? The early feminism of the overtly sexist games world, where I've fought (and won) my battles to have at least as many female characters as male in my games? Or the late feminism of the subtly sexist world of novels, where I find myself deliberately writing books without love stories, with more massacres, riots and fucking, so as to avoid those feminine covers?

For myself, I prefer games. I prefer a world where the sexism can be pointed out, frowned over. Where, sometimes, people apologize for it, maybe even try to change it. I prefer that to the publishers sadly shaking their heads and repeating, 'Men don't buy books written by women.'

I don't want to be in the women's silo. I want to work hard, and long, and know that in the end I'll be judged by the same criteria as a man. I want to know that my work has the same chance of being considered 'important'. That no one's going to stick a flower on the front of it just because I have a vagina. And there's more chance of that happening in games than in novels.

2

Tahmima Anam

Things Your Mama Never Told You (for fear you would demand a sex change)

The world is unequal. Throughout your childhood, through your teens and for most of your twenties, you will believe the world is a generally good place to be a girl. You will do better than boys in school; you will be smarter, more articulate and more interesting. When you reach adolescence, people will start to treat you like a grown-up. In contrast, the boys in your class will be busy fighting and farting through their teens. They will smell bad. They will mumble when spoken to, and treat their limbs as if foreign objects, flinging them about like harpoons and breaking things. However, at some point, probably between college and your first job, you will realize that the cards are stacked against you. It may start with a very small thing, for instance being interrupted at a meeting at work; or something quite significant, such as the discovery that your salary is less than your male counterpart's. Men will take up more space, and breathe more oxygen than you. You will let them, to avoid appearing butch, or even worse, aggressive. You will start to see the world differently, and realize that every moment of your life, every experience has been coloured and influenced by your gender.

You will continue to love men and be attracted to men. Men are wonderful. They are powerful, gorgeous creatures. They sail through life with elan, luxuriating in confidence. If you are heterosexual, you will be attracted to them no matter what bruises they may have inflicted on you in the past, and you will crave partnership and commitment and engagement with them for all the days of your life.

At some point you will become someone's wife. Note, I did not say, 'At some point, you will get married.' Becoming someone's wife is very different from getting married. It can happen at any time in a heterosexual relationship. It happens when you start to take over the domestic responsibilities of the house. You will start doing the laundry and the dishes and handling the household bills. You will organize your and your husband/boyfriend/partner's social life. You will throw parties in which you will cheerfully entertain all the guests and refill their wine glasses and discreetly take their plates from the table at the end of the meal. You will be involved in your husband/boyfriend/partner's work. You will encourage him and big him up and make him face every day with newfound confidence. You will praise him and make him feel good all the time. You will do all of this while also maintaining your own life and your own career.

*

When you have children, you will have to be their mother. When you have children, you cannot be the gregarious, occasional influence who swoops in and makes everything brighter and more fun. You will be the baby's host before it is born; your body will have to bring it into the world, and your body will feed it and keep it alive. Later, you will be responsible for organizing childcare and ensuring there is enough food in the house to feed yourself, your partner and your children. You will be in love. It will be blissful, euphoric, incandescent, but also exhausting, debilitating and life-altering. There is no equivalent in a man's life, no event that will categorically change his relationship to his body, his work, family and identity. This is a journey that you will love. But if you choose to embark on it, you will have no choice of roles. You will have to play the mother.

You cannot be angry. You will want to be angry. If you are angry, you will be called An Angry Young Woman, or worse, An Angry Old Woman, or even worse, An Angry Feminist. You will be called a bitch. You will take comfort in the company of your women friends, but sometimes you will feel painfully, irreparably alone. This will happen to you whether or not you are in a loving relationship with a man. Treating men like the enemy is going to get you nowhere; at least, not the individual men who are your intimates; instead, you will collaborate, invent, learn, grow and octopus your way through life.

In Japan, men read pornography on the subway. Nuff said.

Your female friendships will keep you sane. You will be tempted to spend all your time sucking up to/sleeping with/worshipping/trying to please men. But your women friends will pick you up after you have a break-up or gain weight or lose your job or go through a dry spell with your husband or have a miscarriage or start the menopause. Without them, you might possibly go mad, or accept more compromise than you should, or take a hard line you shouldn't, or forget that you are a clever, magical being with a boundless capacity for love.

If this is your world, you are lucky. If these are your problems, you are unaccountably fortunate. If you grew up in poverty, in a war-torn country, in a feudal society, in Saudi Arabia or Yemen or South Sudan, you will know that being a woman compounds and multiplies any horrors you might face in your life. Your body will be vulnerable to abuse, mutilation and the sex trade. If you want to go to school, you will be hunted down and shot. If there is a war, you will be raped and your daughters and your mother and your grandmother will be raped. You will go hungry, be denied an education, and have no control over who you marry. Your life as a wife will consist of servitude and violence and non-consensual sex. You will be fed lies about this being your lot as a woman, and worse, when you have daughters, you will find yourself repeating this lie to your daughters because by the time they are born you will have no choice but to believe it.

Every day of your life is an opportunity to reverse the long and ugly history of inequality that has dogged our existence since the dawn of time.

'Women are the only
exploited group in history to have
been idealized into powerlessness'

3

Lisa Appignanesi

Fifty Shades of My Own ...

When I was growing up in French Canada, Simone de Beauvoir and Jean-Paul Sartre were the Bacall and Bogie of the intellectual firmament, two radiant stars of the Latin Quarter who stood for the daring life – a perpetual symposium of sex, subversion and philosophy. Not that I actually read *The Second Sex* until I was a graduate student in the UK.

One of the many things I learned as I argued with that cool, analytic, Olympian voice of hers was that, like the curvaceous Jessica Rabbit, the way we're drawn affects what we are. Women, like men, are made, not born. We're at the mercy of our descriptions. These often pre-date our arrival on the scene. To put it another way – from a little base of biology, humans elaborate who they are through their writing, culture, politics and institutions. For women's lives to change, it was important to take more of that power of description into our own hands. The descriptions would hardly ever be uniform, we would disagree with one another vehemently, but at least they wouldn't all come from our colonizers. We would populate the world with our own ideas of what it means to be woman (and man).

The lesson served me well even many years later when I was working on *Mad, Bad and Sad,* my history of women and the mind doctors. Women had long been confined within psychiatric classifications made from the outside: inevitably we had also sometimes played into these categories and expressed our states in the language or gestures given to us. Creatures of word and image, we humans are after all made and remade by our descriptions, sometimes even driven mad by them, boxed into shapes and shoes we think we choose but which make us topple. These descriptions sometimes woo us and render us unaware of the subtleties of the more charming forms of sexism – 'Oh darling, you're too beautiful for (your own) words . . . That inner goddess will wilt after all those hours in the lab, which will also take you away from the children. So let us men get on with finding those pharmaceuticals to treat PMT or anxiety or reproductive problems . . . and set the agenda for science.'

A great deal has changed for women in the course of my lifetime, much of it for the better and not a little of it linked to feminism, self-declared or not. Here and elsewhere, there are more women in public and professional positions – the universities, the law, medicine, NGOs, finance, business, even politics and science, which have so much of our time's descriptive power. We contribute far more widely than ever to the setting of the social agenda, and not only on issues that pertain directly to women, children and the family. If there is less taste for war in the West, if men both feel and are able to admit its horror and their all-too-human vulnerability, that too may be partly linked to the increasing number of female voices in the public arena.

That said, a great deal remains to be done. I can only highlight one area here that has troubled me of late and has almost, on occasion, had me wishing that free expression was not so fundamental to our democracies. I have written at greater length elsewhere about how pornography on the web, readily available to the very young as well as those who can reach the top shelf, has shaped women's bodies and all our sexual relations in insidious ways. It is a noxious and powerful *form of description*. Exaggerated, maimed, disfigured, ever-ready for sex, female bodies put on virtual display have cauterized our growing boys to the living reality of laughing, talking, individual women. Pornography engenders a fantasy of control and pornographers have done much to purvey the notion that satisfaction, like a purchased high, is quick, easy and desirable, part of a supermarket of plenty, ever accessible to choice.

Such images have also helped to induce imitation in girls, who post self-abasing images on social sites, as well as casual copycat violence among teens. Domestic abuse has increased, as has a 'hipster sexism', which for all its ironies is still deeply misogynist. Individual women bear the brunt of donning those fuck-me shoes, as disabling as bound feet, and having surgical make-overs, even of private parts. They masquerade in the guise of these supposedly desirable porn queens and pretend – if heterosexual – that the size of a dick and that swooning inner goddess are all they ever have on their mind. There are category errors at play here: one could say these representations are neither of women nor of men. But because they look like them – just as automata, or androids or zombies in the movies look like humans – we've allowed them to take over our sexual imaginations.

Which is why to my surprise – and perhaps to yours – I found a little part of myself cheering the sudden rampant success of the dire-in-style but wonderfully enthusiastic *Fifty Shades of Grey*. A book that has been read by over 40 million women, many of them mums, can't be dismissed without a little investigation.

One way of thinking about the book's popularity is that it has given women, who ever seem to be more turned on by words than images, a soft porn of their own to counterbalance men's addiction to the web. The written has the distinct advantage that it doesn't feed on an exploitative and abusive sex industry.

Then, too, for all its BDSM, torture toys and pages of contractual negotiations, *Shades* is far more emphatically a popular romance than it is *Story of O*. Dishy and Croesus-rich Grey may indeed woo hapless Ana into his Red Room of Pain and try to dominate her in his subterranean sphere of total control and silent subservience. But he's no Angela Carter Bluebeard. Like any old-fashioned hero of romance, or indeed like Jane Eyre's Rochester, Grey is ultimately better at being tamed by our heroine than he is at dominating her – except when it's for her own pleasure. He's wounded in his masculinity and has even himself been a submissive. *Shades* is really old-fashioned Mills & Boon/Harlequin fantasy, spun out at great length and with more naming of parts. Those romances quietly sell millions too. Women, *pace* Germaine Greer, just seem to be turned on by attentive love . . . however many guises that might wear.

But why this modish wrap of BDSM, whose toys have infiltrated the visual imagination through film and the web? Is it that in our permissive, pornographic West, it's difficult to know any longer what really excites us? Submission to an authority – like Grey, who at the start of the book briefly seems to *know* where that excitement lies – may still some of our worries about having to determine what it is one actually wants. So *Shades* soothes and consoles like most romance. If the heroine wants Grey to know what she wants, she determinedly, at the end of book one, also wants to be free – or at least to maintain an illusion of her freedom.

Well, it's hardly great and profound literature but it is one more description. And it is by a woman. Though I'm glad Hilary Mantel is there as well to be wicked and wise about more Machiavellian spheres.

'Coitus can scarcely be said
to take place in a vacuum; although of
itself it appears as a biological and physical activity,
it is set so deeply within the larger context of
human affairs that it serves as a charged microcosm
of the variety of attitudes and values to
which culture subscribes'

Kate Millet

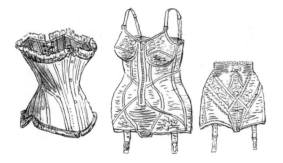

Posy Simmonds

4
Joan Bakewell

If I Couldn't be a Man, I'd be a . . .

At the age of seven I wanted to be a boy . . . The reasons were all around to see. My father went out, he went to work and he went abroad. He was the breadwinner. His life had direction, purpose, adventure. My mother stayed in, went to the shops. Her life lacked direction: she drifted, and she grew depressed. Was she the breadloser?

Men ran the world: they belonged to things out there – the priesthood, football clubs, Parliament, trade unions, the Masons. Women, the women I knew, kept close. To home, to children, to the chores. If in their hearts they belonged to something or somewhere, they didn't share it and it didn't show.

OK, so if I couldn't be a man I'd be a nun. This was no religious impulse, though I did admire the flowing robes and the scrubbed faces. I wanted to avoid the dichotomy the world offered: to be with the men or with the women. I would be de-sexed and live with others like myself. It was an early impulse towards some sort of sisterhood. All this before I was ten.

Then I grew up. But the divisions persisted. In the 1940s I went to a girls' grammar school divided into houses with names meant to encourage: Slessors, Austens, Brontës, Beales, Gaskells and Nightingales. I went on to an all-women college, Newnham, at a time when twelve out of fourteen Cambridge colleges were for men only. I read Simone de Beauvoir. Later I would read Betty Friedan, Germaine Greer, Margaret Drabble, Fay Weldon, but Simone de Beauvoir was the first. It made total sense. I recognized all she said. I was living in the female half of the world: how did you make it across to the other side?

The golden girl of my Cambridge generation, the Zuleika Dobson of her day, Sasha Moorsom was beautiful, self-possessed and brilliant. But asked in a student magazine of the 1950s to write her *Who's Who* entry thirty years hence, she wrote: 'She has been a modest wife to her famous husband.' She became a BBC producer and married the sociologist and political visionary Michael Young. In the early 1960s I met the poet Sylvia Plath and was overawed by her shining American confidence. But her talent meshed with that of her poet husband Ted Hughes. Clearly the matter of male power and women's relationship to it was work in progress.

It still is. I have tried to shape my life according to my own preferences rather than those of the world at large. I have tried, like many of my generation – perhaps like every generation – to defy the conventions of the world into which I was born. I have been lover, wife, mother, broadcaster, journalist, divorcee, grandmother, citizen, novelist, struggling to combine many identities without cracking under the strain. I have also battled male entitlement, resentment, laziness and indifference. I have relished every phase of a long life but there's no denying it has sometimes been tough.

Nonetheless, throughout eight decades I have watched the role of women moving always towards a new configuration. In Britain I have seen laws bring in maternity leave, subsidized childcare, the right of single women to take out mortgages, permissions for abortion, and women priests. Where once their presence was unthinkable, women have moved into new roles and to the top: in the law, the police, medicine, business, as Prime Minister, heads of government departments, universities, as Speaker of the Commons, director of the Royal Institution and heads of City companies. As time goes on, women individually achieve astonishing things. This has happened within living memory – mine – and the changes go on. All that feels good.

But overarching change is achingly slow. I had hoped the Equal Pay Act of 1970, the Sex Discrimination Act of 1975 and Article 141 of the EC Treaty would mark a great leap forward. But we are still legislating for the same thing: 2007, the Gender Equality Duty, 2010, the Equality Act. There are still major systemic failures that survive from a lack of public will. Most conspicuous among them is the matter of money. Women are simply not paid – not valued – as men are. Women in broad-casting know this personally: in the 1960s when I began as a presenter of the BBC Television programme called *Late Night Line-Up* I was paid less than each of its male presenters. This being the liberated sixties, my male colleagues spoke up about the injustice to the editor and my pay increased. But decades later, into the new century, Sue MacGregor, co-presenter of BBC Radio's *Today* programme, discovered she too was being paid less than her colleagues. Certainly the high hopes with which we greeted Barbara Castle's 1970s legislation have been deeply disappointed.

When it began in the late sixties and the seventies, the new feminism was focused and united. Since then the way we live has changed and diverted our attention. Life choices have proliferated and offered us enticing and distracting options. Body issues have come to divide opinion among women: tattoos, cosmetic surgery, the diet industry, the extravagance of fashion and pop culture. Madonna and Lady Gaga should surely be feminist icons, but their images sit oddly beside Charlotte Brontë and Emmeline Pankhurst. All this gives the popular press a chance to mock women as not knowing what they want, and wanting divergent things.

Of course, we want different things ... whether it's cupcakes, a Brazilian, the chance to vote or to wear the burqa. At the same time, a growth of tolerance and non-judgemental morality has tempted us into choices that once would have been taboo: atheism, infidelity, serial marriage, bisexuality, porn, drugs, self-harm. Rows have broken out between women about boob jobs, drinking, pornography and magazine exploitation. We are diverse; we are multifarious; but we are all women.

In the 1880s feminism – or 'the woman question', as it was referred to then – concentrated on education. In the early twentieth century the single issue was the vote. But feminism isn't a single issue any more. It is nothing less than a change to history. It is the most fundamental shift in human consciousness since Darwin's natural selection, the recalibration of humanity worldwide. It is a long slow process like the movement of the earth's crust. Like the tectonic plates it will buck and shudder. But it cannot come to an end. It cannot be written off. We are, after all, half the human race.

'One is not born a woman, one becomes one'

Simone de Beauvoir

5

Camila Batmanghelidjh

Wonderbra

I could write about my big boobs and voluminous hips; the fact that I love the lick of a luscious lipstick and the nous of good nail varnish. I could tell you that I wouldn't be first choice for a Ryvita advert, and that, often, I am defined in terms of what I look like. I hear the tuts of my stiletto-wearing sisters, who look down on my squidgy Crocs and bemoan my lack of a chichi mini-handbag. Fat chance of me fitting into the stereotype of an acceptable female.

Bin the calorie counter! I can't be bothered with that level of the debate because, for me, the essence of being a female resides in a different paradigm.

I have a lot in common with the ferocious twelve-year-old I first met when I founded Kids Company. She was one of the children we supported through our care programmes, a representative for the 1.5 million invisible British children who are being maltreated and whose needs are repeatedly denied by the empathy-deficient. As a twelve-year-old she endeavoured to care for her three younger siblings though prostitution. Both her parents were addicts. The children had not been to school for two years, and they slept in the twelve-year-old's bed, looking to her for protection and care. I admired her so much for the way she had understood an essential task: the necessity of loving and nurturing her siblings. Her aspiration to care represented a personal and ethical ideal by which she was driven: something beautiful she treasured amid the rot. The twelve-year-old and I, coming from completely different backgrounds, had discovered a passion for kindness.

As a child, I tuned into the aesthetics of care – not driven by maltreatment but because I had a grandfather who was a paediatrician. In delivering care to his patients, he had acquired a graceful presence, as beautiful as a painting; as delicate as a soaring bird; as integrated as a flying acrobat. He had all the exquisite precision of a mathematical sum. Across different fields, there is a thematic principle of aesthetics that can best be described as the 'pinnacle of quality' in that particular area. So whether it's being the best doctor, the best fashion designer, the best artist, teacher or carpenter, what unites all these individual functions across disparate fields is the moment of excellence. Excellence crosses the boundaries of any area and becomes an über-experience, the closest definition of which is beauty. For me, endeavouring to touch beauty through the delivery of good-quality care became a vocation.

I believe the best of femininity is expressed by compassionate care. I'm not referring to vagina and penis differentiations; it's an archetype carried by all genders. The feminine intuition identifies the care task, and there is a requirement for the masculine to protect: together, they catalyse the journey towards excellence.

Excellence has a waiting room. You never get there, but

while in the waiting room, you're charged with an energy that allows you a return. So whereas care has always been perceived as a function that depletes the self, I feel caring for others replenishes.

Women are often defined by what their boobs do, whether it's to titillate or to feed. But I reckon there's another kind of boob no one really talks about. It's when care is exchanged between two human beings. Concretely it's called attachment; symbolically it's about an exchange between the caregiver and care recipient, through which both are transformed and enhanced with kindness. Reciprocity is the limousine I sit in, and tangoing with compassion is the feminine principle I aspire to, while getting drunk on a thirst for excellence! So, in short, I'm a drunken whore with alternative boobs! Is that feminist enough for you?

6

Bidisha

The Red Room

Just like Christian Grey, the toxic abuser – sorry, dashing lead – of *Fifty Shades of Self-Hate*, I have my own secret Red Room of Pain. In the secret room I file every example of woman-hating I have experienced or witnessed, large or small: the harassment, the mistreatment, the violation, discrimination, unwanted touching, injustice, belittling, victim-blaming, casual 'jokes' that are really insults, marginalization, objectification, patronage. Everything from the rapes and beatings, the sudden attacks and long-hidden abusive relationships, to the work meetings in which I see women being talked over, interrupted, subtly undermined or openly put down. I keep a log of the abusers I know, every one of whom got away with it and has a public reputation as 'a really nice guy'. I even trap the silence of those who, when a woman speaks, simply look over her head and ignore it.

In the room I stock everything from the beauty, diet, fashion and surgery adverts encouraging us to make ourselves ever more artificial, self-obsessed and doll-like to the damning statistics showing how few women are represented as powerful and knowledgeable experts in the media, how few are appointed to the best jobs, how few women artists are credited and rewarded for their genius, how few are paid equally or given meaningful opportunities, acknowledged as pioneers and remembered by history. I archive the manifold stereotypes and base insults, the jibes and jokes. I put in those subtle moments when the mere mention of a woman results in a snort, a snigger and a rolling of the eyes.

I never forget those details. I've been a feminist all my life because society's scathing contempt for women, its exploitation of women for underpaid and under-acknowledged menial, caring, sexual and administrative labour, the ubiquitous and endemic violence against women and the leniency towards abusers of women are completely and utterly obvious. What is more painful than anything is some women's internalization of this hatred: their harsh and brittle judgement of themselves and each other. In a patriarchy, both sexes are brought up to behave the same: to worship men and deride women.

Many things have changed for women in the last fifty years – but much has remained the same and so much still needs to be done. Desperate times call for feminist measures and we are currently in the middle of great change, challenge and activism. The age of revolution has returned, grass-roots feminism has proliferated and there is an inspiring outrage and energy, spurred by issues both old and new. Our concern about relatively recent social, economic and cultural shifts is combined with frustration that long-standing battlegrounds are still live, and galled disbelief that we are having to make the same arguments over and over again – like pointing out that a rape survivor is never responsible in any way for a man deciding to rape her.

We are concerned about the pornification of culture, the

mainstreaming of the sexploitation industry, the sexualization of girl children, the sharp increase in cosmetic surgery including labioplasty, the commonness of abusive relationships among the young and the normalization (among both sexes) of the abuse, coercion, violation and control of young women by their boyfriends. We are concerned that in the fight over abortion rights the fundamental understanding that a woman has the right and the intelligence to decide what happens with her own body will be lost. We are concerned about trafficking – which involves kidnapping, deception, violent physical and mental brutalization, traumatization and constant rape – and about the wider assumption that it is OK for a man to pay a human woman for sex, as though he's ordering a drive-through meal or renting a DVD. Women are not objects to be bought, sold, used and abused by men.

We are concerned about female genital mutilation, 'honour' killing, forced marriage, including child marriage, rape as a weapon of war and a perk of peace and the infinite rape myths, victim-blaming and perpetrator excusal, which have resulted in 90 per cent of rapes going unreported and only 6 per cent of the remaining 10 per cent resulting in a rape conviction in the UK, which is not a war zone and has a legal framework for prosecuting rape yet still cannot bring itself to punish rapists.

We are concerned about the media vilification and sabotage of those few women in power, the reality and resilience of the glass ceiling and women's many unpaid, expected and unacknowledged labours away from the office. Women in families take care of children and elders because the men in families do not.

Thanks wholly to feminism we now have a language, a vision, an understanding and an analysis to apply to our pain. What we need now is for the perpetrators to stop. The oppressors are not winning by cleverness or sophisticated rhetoric but by sheer force, by the violent leverage of brutal power – and shame on them for that. The question of gender is not very complicated: treat women as you would be treated, because we are people, human beings with minds and names, ideas, talents, real lives. If you would not like to be raped, harassed, ignored, patronized, treated as stupid, judged by your age and appearance or used only for the cheap, nasty and repetitive labour you can give, don't do that to others.

I remind myself during moments of activist fatigue and flagging faith that the women's movement is the longest and most successful peaceful human-rights fight in world history. The resistance we encounter is a sign that we are on the right path and that our words have hit a raw nerve. Those who react with vociferous derision when they are called on their misogyny are enraged because their cover has been blown, their presumption of superiority has been questioned and women have dared to challenge them and answer back.

Those who say that women are their own worst enemies or that feminists are in disagreement about core issues are lying. There are more than fifty shades of feminism, but they're fifty shades of the same colour: red. Not grey, that in-between yuppie hue of prevarication, indecision and relativism. Feminism is coloured the red of women's rage, women's despair, women's power, women's brilliance and women's ability to survive. It is the lifeblood of emancipation, which pulses with never-ending faith that freedom and justice are only ever a heartbeat away.

'There are no dangerous thoughts.
Thinking is dangerous itself'

Hannah Arendt

7
Lydia Cacho

Not in the Name of Love

The first time I understood my body was mine, I was seven years old. It was 1970. My mother caught me masturbating.

'What are you doing?' she asked.

Since I had no reason not to, I answered bluntly.

'Feeling good,' I said.

My mum sat down next to me. She began telling me how marvellous it was to be born a girl. She explained that I was touching my clitoris and my vulva. At the end of her simple elucidation, she made it clear that my body was mine and no one could or should ever tell me otherwise. My mother was a French feminist psychologist, my brothers, sisters and I were lucky to have her as an educator in Catholic Mexico, surrounded as we were by a relentlessly sexist, pro-macho society.

When the time came, my mother and I talked about eroticism, desire and sharing my pleasure and my body with other people. Being a skinny, strong-minded teenager who doubted the existence of God and hated 'girly stuff', all this was no easy matter. In my family we used to hug and kiss a lot. We shared feelings honestly and all opinions were open for discussion. We negotiated conflicts across the kitchen table. We also all learned to cook and change tyres, to clean the house and use a toolbox. My parents made sure we knew that we weren't an altogether normal Mexican family and we were proud of it.

It was never easy to bring those familial ideas to the outside world. I discovered what an existential crisis was when I found myself wishing I had girlfriends who did not hate their bodies, or who didn't metamorphose themselves into sexual instruments just to get a little affection from boys.

I qualified as a weirdo. Bullies insulted me at school because I didn't succumb to being mistreated or because I challenged those who made sexist remarks about women's bodies and opinions. They called me ugly and eventually they hit me. I had to learn how to handle masculine violence, to learn to decipher the body language of boys when they got angry. I had to learn that their very inability to discuss differences made them physically violent. I kept pointing out that they were nice only if we women obeyed them, and we did so out of fear of rejection.

At an early age I wrote in my diary how predictable most boys were. Without really understanding it, I developed my own tools for confronting a culture that refuses to admit not only what my mother told me when I was little – that my body was mine – but also that it is impossible to establish a real dialogue with someone who does not consider you an equal. If someone thinks of you as property, he will always treat you as an object. If someone buys you as a sex slave, he will always see you as an object without rights. If someone decides you are nothing but an incubator for sperm, your body is no longer your own: it is expropriated and colonized. Your freedom to choose is stolen from you. If someone takes your freedom to choose, you have become a slave of their cultural values. If you are a slave to be sold and bought, people will believe it is just fine for you and other girls to be abused, raped and battered in the name of money or love.

In 2013 'objectification' is an old word with a new, stronger meaning. The little girl in me keeps yelling: *Not in the name of love or freedom*. There has to be another way.

'And of course men know best about everything,
except what women know better'

George Eliot

8

Shami Chakrabarti

Motherhood

My feminism is not rooted in learning and great intellectual tracts – I often wish it were. It is born mostly of observation and experience. My mother died suddenly on the same 2011 day as Amy Winehouse, at just sixty-nine years old. A beautiful, clever and talented woman, her confidence and life chances had been limited at an early age by her traditional Indian bureaucrat father. Both academic and creative opportunities that emerged in her teens had been controlled or cast aside. She wanted better for me and, while nothing and no one is perfect, she achieved it.

I've thought more and more about motherhood in recent years. My mother's, my own and that of so many great women that I have had the privilege to know or watch in my human-rights work.

Doreen Lawrence is a role model and a friend. Who can imagine converting the gravest grief at a child's murder into a campaign to reform the policing and wider societal values of an entire nation? Her calm courage should be an inspiration to everyone. From the worst pain and adversity some strength and purpose may come.

Verna Bryant also lost her child to senseless murder. Her vulnerable daughter Naomi was killed by a man released on licence from prison, with the incompetent authorities neither fully aware of his hideous record of violence against women and girls nor capable of adequately supervising him in the community. A tabloid campaign blamed the murderer's human rights but Verna and wonderful young women lawyers here at Liberty used the positive obligations under the Human Rights Act to trigger a broad inquest and narrative verdict that forced a mirror on professional and institutional failure.

Janis Sharp spent over a decade fighting her son Gary McKinnon's extradition to the United States. He has Asperger's syndrome and developed suicidal thoughts over a decade-long limbo after the American authorities branded him a 'cyber-terrorist' for a search for UFOs that culminated in an embarrassing hack into the Pentagon computer system. Most mothers love their kids no matter what scrapes they get themselves into. Most would fight for their safety. Janis literally took on the British government and US security establishment. Janis fought an illiberal and inhumane extradition law and for once the law didn't win.

Observing the unfailing determination and self-sacrifice of these mothers has been a privilege and an inspiration. But these extraordinary women are far from alone. Mothers everywhere – those who battle to care for their families on poverty-level wages, those who suffer domestic abuse from partners who should be their greatest source of support, and those who give everything in the fight to secure justice for their children – so often step in front of harm in attempting to shield those around them. It is not an easy role to fulfil and none of us ever feel as if we do it perfectly. But though it is often a tough club to be a member of, it is also the most important one in the world.

'When you strike a woman, you strike a rock'

ANC Women's League

9
Jane Czyzselska
My Lesbian Body

I'm going to start and end with my 'lesbian' body. After all, it's me, mine; and yet I feel I lack complete ownership of it. Others own it through expectation. Living in a culture that values hetero-normativity over other lifestyles leaves my body and what I choose to do with it frequently policed by men who feel entitled to silently remind me of the potential consequences of any transgression.

My transgression is twofold: I'm a lesbian who 'looks heterosexual'. My partner looks more 'androgynous' than me, and when I'm with her in public the fact that I'm unavailable to men seems to rule out the possibility of being left alone. We are watched as if performing in public.

Paradoxically some gay men and women consider my gender presentation to be 'not lesbian enough' and often make incorrect assumptions about my political stance, thinking of me as conservative or conventional.

Much of this concerns my clothes, hair and make-up, but my body probably looks similar to many women approaching their mid-forties: healthy but sagging in some places, untamed and untoned through infrequent gym attendance, yet 'unquestionably' female.

I have breasts and a vagina and yet I don't use these contested areas of my body in the way that many women do. I have never breastfed because I don't have nor do I want children. This means that I will never be a 'productive' female but a perpetual rebellious teenager in the eyes of some; and possibly sad and unfulfilled in the eyes of others. But I relish the amount of freedom this gives me to be sensual and sexual and to enjoy the natural world.

The radical queer trans and intersex women and men I know quite literally embody this freedom because they call into question conventional binary-gendered expectations. Some do this by living as women or men, avoiding surgery to alter their bodies and taking hormones.

How does this affect me and my experience of being female? One of the things that's always excited me about acknowledging the intersectionality of gender is that being a woman today has the potential to be manifested in almost any way, despite the cultural and conventional barriers that will always exist. It's this fact that makes it more possible for me to feel freer about my life choices in respect of gender expectations.

Age and experience, personal-development work and an awareness of my inner world all contribute to my growing sense of empowerment, but my body, to paraphrase the feminist artist Barbara Kruger, is still a battleground. In fact it was ever thus.

Before puberty kicked in I was a 'tomboy', eschewing pink or 'girls'' clothes in hopes of being taken more seriously. As a teenager I experienced a period of anorexia which rendered my body more androgynous than nature intended and gave me a sense of agency in a society that felt beyond my control.

Margaret Thatcher, Britain's first female Prime Minister, may have been newly resident in Downing Street, but in my world women didn't seem to have the same status as men did. In my twenties I explored this perceived social inequality further through 'cross-dressing': binding my breasts, stuffing a bottle of Mum deodorant down my men's briefs, sprinkling hair clippings on to my upper lip and working as a nightclub door 'man'. By day, as a young journalist, I had an androgynous look.

Over the years I've come to recognize that my gender exploration has been a rite of passage in a society that quite literally values men more than women (over forty years after the Equal Pay Act, women working full time are still likely to be paid 14.9 per cent per hour less than men) and has only recently begun to regard lesbians as equal in law to heterosexual women. I realize the confusion I've felt about my gendered inner world mirrors the gender confusion and power imbalances experienced by all humans in the world we collectively inhabit. And like many middle-class white women, I feel anger that men are four times as likely to be elected to the UK government. I feel a deep sadness that many women around the world are so insecure in and removed from their natural bodies that they pay surgeons to cut them open and remould them. I feel angry that women in their millions are victims of rape and torture, and extremely fortunate to live in a country where I'm unlikely to experience 'corrective' rape because I'm gay.

I am grateful to have met my gorgeous girlfriend who loves me (and my body, as it is) flaws and all. I feel thankful that I earn a salary in a job that I love, with people I respect, that has permitted me to maintain the privilege of having a mortgage with a credit rating that enables me to have choices. I mention this because I'm aware that my class and the colour of my skin have a significant bearing on how I am able to engage with and negotiate the world.

Finally, I am grateful to be in my lesbian body today because I feel good in it, most of the time, and because it feels primed to respond to a woman's touch. And, crucially, living in London as an openly gay woman – unlike the lesbians in St Petersburg, Kampala or even some areas of Britain, where homosexuality is considered sinful – I experience a corporeal safety that is easy to take for granted.

IO

Sayantani DasGupta

Can Sisterhood be Global? Fifty Shades of Transnational Feminism

'They want to see how oppressed we brown women are.'

We are in the faculty club of an elite New York City academic institution, before my mother is to give a talk based on her latest book, *Mothers for Sale: Women in Kolkata's Sex Trade*. Based on hundreds of interviews with women in Kolkata's red-light district (Sonagachi), the book records sex workers telling of their own lives in their own words. As such, it stands in contrast to projects like the Academy Award-winning 2004 documentary *Born into Brothels,* which in many ways cast director Zana Briski in the role of 'white rescuer' of Sonagachi children, and sex workers as 'evil mothers'.

The audience is packed, and at first I am thrilled. But then my mother reminds me of the complexities of publicly speaking about women's oppression in our communities; complexities that cast a shadow on any facile notions of a global feminist sisterhood.

When my Indian immigrant mother joined the 1970s main-stream feminist movement, she was the only woman of colour, and one of a few married women in her graduate-school 'consciousness raising group'. The assumption was that she must be 'oppressed' by both her 'arranged' marriage and motherhood. Forget that she had a fabulous partnership with my father, and considered motherhood central to her progressive politics; clearly, she was an oppressed brown woman!

I grew up alongside my mother's feminist consciousness. With critiques of mainstream feminism's race, class and national politics came her organizing in immigrant communities. My mother eventually founded Manavi, the first south Asian anti-domestic-violence organization in the US. Although she also continues to work with mainstream anti-domestic-violence organizations, she always reminds me of the complexities of speaking out about gender-based violence in immigrant communities. To do so is to walk the razor's edge between mainstream conceptions about 'our [read: backward] cultures' and the resistance of an immigrant 'model minority' community against racist forces all too ready to demonize it.

Consider the work of *New York Times* reporter Nicholas Kristof, including the PBS film *Half the Sky: Turning Oppression into Opportunity for Women* which he produced with his wife Sheryl WuDunn, alongside the book of the same name. While the film brings gender violence, including rape, coerced sex work and genital cutting, to international attention, it simultaneously reinforces racist/imperialist assumptions by focusing solely on Asian and African countries (India, Somalia, Kenya, Thailand, etc.). While a few passing comments acknowledge that gender violence exists everywhere, the point that is reiterated through the film is that gender oppression is 'worse' in 'these countries' – that it is indeed a part of 'their culture'. Such voyeuristic 'rescue' narratives, which teach 'us' about an oppressed 'them', only reinforce global North-South divides rather than bridging them.

Such missteps can also come from efforts at inclusion. My mother and I once went to see a series of diverse monologues on gender violence by a feminist playwright I admire. In one monologue, a tattooed Irish redhead in a leather vest described buying a gun to revenge herself on her rapist. Yet, in the very next, a south Asian actress delivered her lines in a headscarf, shrieking mournfully, a send-up of every stereotype of the passive veiled woman. This pattern seemed consistent. Only white women fought back. We brown women were just busy being oppressed.

Many years ago, my mother and I were on a women's conference panel alongside Egyptian activist/physician/writer Nawal El Saadawi. At that time, Pratibha Parmar and Alice Walker had just made *Warrior Marks*, a film about female genital cutting. Dr El Saadawi made a powerful point that day. She wished Western-based feminists would stop speaking about the issue (and calling it female genital mutilation, or FGM). She argued that they were rendering real resistance to genital cutting by African/Middle Eastern feminists ineffective. Local feminists had to fight against the perception that their activism was somehow a part of an imperialist Western project rather than resistance to a cultural practice *from within*. The best support Western feminists could give their global sisters, she said, was to listen first and speak later, following the lead of and partnering with local feminists, giving economic and other support from a position of 'solidarity' rather than 'saving'.

In many ways, feminism itself has been used as a weapon against women of the global South. Cultural critic Gayatri Chakrovorty Spivak coined the term 'white men saving brown women from brown men' to describe the imperialist use of women's oppression as justification for political aggression. And we have seen reflections of this dynamic in the way that the US has justified wars in Afghanistan and Iraq as missions to 'free Islamic women from the veil'. (See here Lila Abu-Lughod's article 'Do Muslim Women Really Need Saving?'.)

When Robin Morgan edited *Sisterhood Is Global* in 1996, the assumption that there was one 'international women's movement' was already coming under critique. Women from the global South were being claimed as sisters by feminists of the global North, but this claim was of discursive diversity only – there was no real recognition of how economic globalization, imperialism, xenophobic immigration policies and the like were inextricable from any understanding of women's rights in these communities.

Real sisterhood – a sisterhood of solidarity rather than saving – can perhaps only come from a place of inward looking; a place where we are willing to listen, critique our own expectations and assumptions – how our own privileges lead to other women's exploitations – and be unafraid to constantly evolve and change.

Recently, on the tumblr site 'oppressedbrowngirlsdoingthings', next to awesome images of hijab-wearing women on skateboards I saw a fabulous photo: a sari-clad, grey-haired Indian granny wearing flip-flops while driving a huge motorcycle.

In moving the feminist legacies of our foremothers forward, let us draw from such diverse strengths. My sari-clad feminist foremothers may not have ridden motorbikes, but they did leave me a heritage of complexity and intersectionality, self-critique and social change, conscious collaboration rather than unexamined allegiance.

Laura Dockrill

Today. Do i feel like a 'woman'? It's only just blown my mind tha

without filling in an application form or going on a training

will have the same ability - to create something new all over

world like toys... or food... or else i'll go mad.

bottle out LOUD in a french accent, do i feel like a Women

A-N-Y-T-Hing. Do i maybe feel like a woman then?

with huge overbearing sloppy tentacles, taking up every corner

¿Sometimes. Sometimes people are frightened of women...

Secrets and opinions i am too scared to share in case i mess up

are just not valid? I want to feel like a poster.

pair of stilts. I want to fee like Helena Bonham carter's hair

How to hold a babies head. To pack a picnic basket. To care

be hold. To talk. To whisper. to laugh it off. to scream.

to fix, to undo, to look out. Mostly you feel like you're

~~yoga~~ class. Doing anything not

universe snuggled up with X-factorettes and the dregs of

about calories. Mostly you are reserving yourself.

doing. Taking care of the swelling gas of confidence

you look for when you most need it and it lends

pROud. But never too proud to say 'ouch.' When ~~all~~ I've

I've done it. when i complain to the ~~~~ fully dressed

I know that's how women end up HERE ← or when an

contact with you, you realise you used to do this to

you used to do, palming off the responsibility, designatio

of peoples handbags, dividing up the perishable goods

cuddles. You notice then, that you have, accidently, not on

woman when i'm doing jobs that are stereotypically for men

damp. Logical rather than emotional. I am proud to be in

And when i look as though i've been

I can grow something inside me. I can do that. For free.

course. And that thing that I grow, if all going to plan
again. like a set of Russian dolls. I have to see the
when I am reading the ingredients of the shampoo
? When I flirt with people - women, men, animals...
Do I want to be like Ursula from The little mermaid
every cranny I know.

Sometimes I feel like a hen, on a collection of story egg
offend. upset. Embarrass. Belittle. or perhaps that they
I want to feel like a sword. I want to feel like a
What about when I know what to do? My instinct.
To nurture. To embrace. To protect. To frown. To
To know what's best, to trust myself. To look in,
trying not to feel like the only fat arse in the
get caught in the stingy armpit of the GMTV
big Brother orphanages, talking heads nibbling on
icely. or pretending you know what you are
t you hold in the pit of your belly that sometimes
n back an 'Out of office.' The woman is very
de a proper chicken stock. from scratch, I know
ff at the gym, with my boobs out. shameless.
aid person on public transport makes eye
Other women for reassurance, just like
a leader. You will be sharing out the rations
an emergency. That's YOUR job. Handing out
purpose become a woman. I feel mostly like a
unblocking a drain, removing a nice wall of rising
tune with my harmony, listening to the weather
rying. They are not tears. they are just sequins.

II

Lynne Featherstone

Political Women

I got sacked from my first job.

It was a small company, and one night during my six-week trial period one of the managers asked if I would join him and a blue-chip client for the showreel and drinks. Afterwards he offered me a lift home, insisted on stopping for a drink on the way and, as he dropped me at my mother's house, made a pretty crude lunge at me. I told him where to go – and the next day I was fired.

I sobbed my heart out to my mother – who said it was just one of life's lessons. Thank goodness these days (this was long ago) it isn't just one of life's lessons: it is sexism, bullying and discrimination – and we have laws against it!

My mother was without doubt a feminist. She would have laughed though at such a title. She never viewed it that way – it was just how she lived her life.

I remember her telling me a story about when she and my

father (who died when I was fifteen) were living in Birmingham during the war. He was in the Admiralty and she was working in an office. She said that on the first day there they both came in from work at the same time. My father sat down with pipe and slippers and my mother walked into the kitchen to get dinner ready.

She then walked straight out of the kitchen and said to my father: 'Joe – we both came in from work at the same time. Why should you sit down while I go and get dinner ready? That's not right.' And from then on it was an equal relationship. She wouldn't have termed it feminism; she would have just thought it was logical and common sense – and fair!

I do remember tales she told of her early life. One of two sisters and five brothers, she left school at thirteen and was made to go and work as an apprentice milliner. She absolutely hated it. She also hated having to take her brothers' and her father's lunches to them where they worked. She said that she used to have to take hot soup to them on the top deck of an open-top bus. If the bus stopped suddenly the soup would slop over and run down the window in front of the driver. So she – being a girl – had to serve the males of the family. Perhaps that is where the seeds of her feminism were sown.

She was an amazing woman. She and my father started a post-war electrical DIY business in London, and after my father died she carried it on to be a real success, with ten shops, a head office and a repair and wholesale business. So I grew up never expecting anything other than to work hard and make my way in the world. So did my sister Della. She also started a successful business with her husband Dan – a shop in Goodge Street called Nice Irma's Floating Carpet, selling Indian hangings, waterbeds and beanbags and lots of beautiful and exotic fabrics. And I started my own design business at the age of twenty-seven.

With a role model like my mother I never thought for a single moment that I would be restricted in any way in my future path. It didn't occur to me that being female was even an issue. So I never hesitated to start my own business – because it held no fears for me. It was familiar, in the true sense of the word.

I had only just joined the Liberal Democrats when my mother died. In fact, my sister and I looked after her as she was dying. She would spend the afternoons with me at my house. I remember coming in and telling her I had joined a political party. 'Which one?' she said. 'Liberal Democrats,' I said. 'Yuk,' she said. At the time of her death she voted Conservative but she had come from communist roots in her youth and had she lived, of course, by now she would definitely be a Liberal Democrat.

It makes me very sad that she died before I really got going in politics, but as I have progressed through from local councillor to London Assembly member to MP and now government minister, it has been that grounding in being yourself, thinking for yourself and believing that you can achieve anything if you are willing to commit to it and work flat out that has steered me all the way through – and an unswerving belief in equality.

In my previous portfolio as a Home Office minister and Equalities minister, my early feminist roots came to good purpose. In my portfolio I had women and domestic violence, and I was also appointed ministerial champion for tackling violence against women and girls internationally – a role I retain to this day, together with my new role as Parliamentary Under-Secretary in the Department of International Development.

What I see – from the United Kingdom right across the world – is a spectrum of oppression and violence against women.

In my own country there are still two women a week killed by their partners or ex-partners, and one in four women experiences domestic violence in her lifetime. Many women are left with children and have to bring them up – often on their own (including me). Over forty years after the Equal Pay Act, there is still a far too large pay gap. And there are career women still thwarted in their path to the top by old-boy networks.

And as I work across the world I see women who experience the worst that can be imagined – rape as a weapon of war, social norms where violence is an accepted way of life; and too many places where women have no rights, no power and little hope.

Where there are no laws we must pursue their introduction. Where there are laws we must fight for them to be properly enforced. And where there is violence we must end impunity. Women across the world need economic empowerment, land and property rights, fairness, justice and freedom from violence.

I am passionate about all of this. I cannot bear injustice. And perhaps that is what has brought me to the role I am in today.

And when I look back at my history, I can see my own continuum and must say a heartfelt thank-you to my mother. She wasn't easy on me or my sister – but her example and her strength of character run through our veins.

'There never will be complete
equality until women themselves help
to make laws and elect lawmakers'

Susan B. Anthony

12

Carlene Firmin

Wifey, Sket, Hoodrat

Over the past five years I've interviewed hundreds of gang-associated women and girls – wives of gang members, girl-friends, sisters, mothers and cousins. These are women who've been victimized and involved in the victimization of others. While each of their stories and experiences is unique, they share painfully consistent tales of inequality, abuse and fear, combined with a sense that their choices are not their own.

These are girls who, having committed serious and some-times violent offences, are told, 'Since you're behaving like the boys, we're going to treat you like the boys.' As a result these girls-behaving-like-boys are supported in male-dominated serv-ices by professionals who have little or no experience working with women and girls. These are women who, having accessed domestic-abuse services, are afraid to tell professionals about the extent of their gang association in case they're perceived as unworthy victims; and are then held responsible for the abusive situations they face. Even though the levels of violence to which these women and girls are exposed are extreme, the broader context of inequality that they seek to navigate smacks of the discrimination faced by women and girls around Britain on a daily basis. And while it is true that the situation for many women of all ages in the UK has improved over the past fifty years, for others the violence they experience has become ever more complicated. It is intertwined with criminal gangs, perpetrated by their peers, and facilitated by all manner of mobile-phone technology and social media.

'Link' or 'wifey'?' 'Sket' or 'good girl'? 'Hoodrat' or 'dime'? Such are the labels pasted on young women in the twenty-first century. These are labels that have influenced my choices, world-view and self-perception over the past twenty years. Yes, these are 'tarts', 'sluts' and 'tomboys' wearing twenty-first-century names, and in that sense they are nothing new. But the impact social media and mobile-phone technology have in promulgating and facilitating these epithets has reached seriously damaging proportions.

Not only can a girl now be known as 'easy' (a sket/link) by her peers or her local neighbourhood, but the judgements placed on her go viral, global, and persist for ever on the world-wide web. In addition, women and girls are now stalked and harassed via phones and networking sites. They are relentlessly verbally abused over the phone, and threatened over Twitter. The speed at which such global social judgement has invaded the lives of females who have grown up with cyberspace has rapidly overtaken the policies and services designed to protect them from violence.

The combination of social media and the increasingly violent presence of street gangs is poison. Gang-associated girls are photographed with rival gang members and attacked as punishment, identified and tracked down via their Facebook profiles and named on 'sket lists' that are circulated over phones and web pages alike. They are 'fair game' both online and in person. The risks to their personal safety are serious and very real.

How can we keep gang-affected women and girls safe in a threatening environment that is becoming increasingly difficult to manage and contain?

Having an independent, supportive and determined mother made an indescribable difference to the choices I made as a young woman and the direction I've taken. This is interesting, given that my mother never discussed feminism with me, or identified herself as a feminist. In fact, it is only in this last year that I have become comfortable with the idea that I am a feminist, and have introduced such language and debate into my family home. My mum has welcomed this and she agrees with both the arguments and the language. She, like me, never thought that feminism was something that was accessible to her. To move forward, it's imperative to challenge perceptions of feminism as an exclusive club.

There are women from all walks of life who for all manner of reasons don't feel they would make particularly 'good feminists'. Up until last year my mother and I would have classified ourselves in that group. Like many from a range of backgrounds, we felt disengaged from feminism. It didn't seem to be for *us*. I know young women who still feel that they don't fit into feminism because their heels are too high. For gang-associated women, it's because they've hurt others or have been damaged themselves.

Interrogation has enabled me to see that feminism actually is open to women like me and my mother. I want to ensure that feminism has the space to support women and girls who have been both violent and violated. This is the challenge I want my peers to meet. The lessons from my mother and feminist role models I have met over the past five years have offered me a framework for understanding inequality from which I can hang, conceptualize and understand the experiences of gang-associated women.

As feminism moves into the twenty-first century, it is fundamental that the ever-changing, often violent discrimination that girls and young women are faced with is confronted head-on. Ignoring their experiences only plays into practices of labelling and creates hierarchies of 'deserving' and 'undeserving' women. It isolates some of our most vulnerable. They need support from us all.

13
Lennie Goodings
Immodest Power

Recently a couple of young women, both writers, said to me that it must be wonderful to have the power I have – being a publisher, and particularly being the publisher of Virago. Slightly embarrassed, I ducked the implied compliment. Not because I don't have power, and not because I don't enjoy it either. It is absolutely wonderful to be able to work to real effect. But it seemed unseemly to talk about that power, to admit to it, to claim it. Yet I have worked for powerful women. I publish powerful women and I love and admire powerful women. So why do I demur?

Elaine Showalter poses the problem in terms of women writers, and in an interesting way:

> Women have been too dignified and self-effacing to make their own claims to artistic immortality. Women novelists . . . have rarely produced manifestos, aligned themselves in a

notable school, named their generation (whether Lost or Beat) and their genre, or feuded heroically and publicly.

Are women modest because to be otherwise implies that we are more important, more successful, more effective, than other women? Do we think immodesty will make us unpopular? Or is it that to be a woman with power feels uncomfortable because we think it means we are unusual? Unique, even?

It's true that women are still not properly present at the top of business and government, (in the Church of England!), or in enough decision-making roles. But are women in *power* actually uncommon? I think not. The fact is we are everywhere and in every walk of life: there are thousands of us in law, medicine, business, education, the police, media, even in government. But it's as if that fact has not penetrated into everyday consciousness: women in power are not regarded as ordinary. They are thought of as remarkable and not portraying the usual state of things. Is that why women shy from claiming their position?

The shying away may be because a woman who takes power does it with the knowledge that she will attract comment. Think of the language we use almost exclusively for women in power, the word 'bossy' being the most interesting. Is it bad to be bossy if one is the boss? To be powerful you have to be visible and you have to be immodest. It feels safer, certainly it's nicer and better behaviour, if we wait for the accolades, the attention, the praise, rather than act as if it is our due. It feels better to be part of the crowd.

And here's the rub: who are some of the hardest on the women who put their heads above the parapet? Other women. I have long witnessed this – since the beginning of Virago, in fact – and so have had plenty of time to ponder on it. Women are often the first to claw down other women. I believe this is linked to my original point – that powerful women are not seen as *ordinary*. The prevailing perception seems to be that we are still a rare breed. The result of which is that powerful women are unique. We are seen by other women as representative of all women: every woman who stands up is regarded, at some level, as representing all women.

Other women criticize and detract because they want to dissociate themselves from that representation. 'If that's feminism, I am not a feminist.' 'If that's what a woman in power does, I am not that kind of woman.' 'She doesn't speak for me.' And of course, 'I wouldn't wear *that*.' There is a long and dreadful tradition of mean-girl behaviour, and I suppose jealousy and envy are at play here too. But first and foremost, I think this is about the anxiety of representation. We've seen it before – with black and Asian people, with gay and lesbian groups. It is not an unusual phenomenon when someone from a group represented as a minority raises their head above the parapet.

I am hardly suggesting that women cease to criticize other women. That would be ridiculous. What I am saying is that we can disagree – even vehemently and without that criticism being reduced to mere bitchiness. But we don't need to tear apart another woman's view out of the fear that we are being misrepresented.

Because the truth about women in power, in the Western world at least, is that we're no longer a minority group. It's time to wake up to that, to recognize that we are not all that unusual or unique, and that one of us does not stand for all of us. There is space for lots of different 'shades' of feminism, femaleness and femininity.

And it is also time for women like me to realize that it is not immodest to accept the compliment of being a powerful woman. That it is just an ordinary fact.

'If our history has taught us anything,
it is that action for change directed against
the external conditions of our
oppression is not enough'

Audre Lorde

14
Linda Grant
Past and Present

Sunday, 11 November 2012.

I am reading on my iPad an article in the *Sunday Times* about the poet of the Great War, Edward Thomas. A notification flashes up on the screen that a friend has commented on a photo I uploaded to Facebook the day before. In this photograph, taken on International Women's Day, 1979, I am wearing a boiler suit with a purple chain hanging from belt to knees in a slightly eerie precursor of hip-hop. I am handing out pro-choice leaflets. My arm is around a woman in a calf-length skirt and a blouse with a pussy-cat bow. Although I remember her perfectly well, I don't recall her name. I know she was a lawyer and had dashed out of her office at lunchtime to join the march.

The Facebook comment adds further information: she was American, a graduate of an Ivy League university, who had gone into labour in the college library. The librarian, standing over her, said, 'I knew we shouldn't have admitted women to the university.' I do recall that her son was barmitzvahed around this time, so the complaint in the library would have taken place in the mid-sixties. The International Women's Day march of 1979 was the same year that I tried to open a department-store credit card and was told that the forms needed to be countersigned by a male relative: my husband or, if I was not married, my father.

Returning to read the article about Edward Thomas and the forthcoming commemorative events for the outbreak of the First World War, I reflect that these times, when someone in a position of authority could verbalize the view that women should not be admitted to higher education, or that a woman could not have financial autonomy, seem to me as distant now as the Great War was to us then. Times inconceivable. The carnage of the Front has passed out of living memory. The Europe and North America in which women could be considered unsuitable for education and financial responsibility now exists *only* in memory. I remember it perfectly well. I remember the girl in the year above me at school in 1966, the cleverest, most attractive and vivacious of us all, the star of the Upper Fifth, was forced to leave because she was pregnant. Abortion was illegal; she was sent to a home for unmarried mothers, the baby adopted. From this fate her life never recovered. The Pill became available to unmarried women in Liverpool one year later.

What has feminism accomplished? If you take a utopian view of politics, you might say, very little. Natasha Walter has written, in her book *Living Dolls*, about the pinkification of the lives of girls; how even children have been sexualized. Role models of footballers' wives, page-three models, *X Factor* wannabes still dominate teenage bedrooms. Men rule the boardrooms, politics, broadcasting – wherever there is power, men are squatting on the best positions. Women complain that parenting excludes them from the top jobs. And once we leave the West, we see struggles at the most primitive level for girls to win the right to learn to read.

But the Britain I grew up in is simply unimaginable to girls leaving school in 2013. They would not recognize the assumption that men should be paid more than women because they were the breadwinners and women worked only for pin money (treats). They would be baffled at the idea that out of twenty-seven Oxford colleges, only five admitted women. They would scarcely believe that in a factory women were excluded from training for skilled jobs as machine operators. They would wonder what bat-shit-crazy policy decided that a single woman could not apply for a mortgage.

Equality is in the eye of the beholder. I grew up in the provincial suburbs, where the highest aspiration of a mother was for her daughters to marry. University was for the exceptional, gifted, fluky few, not as clever as boys but far cleverer. Even going to a bluestocking school, the majority of us were pointed to teacher-training college, because teaching was one of the few professions that could be envisaged for girls. These are, of course, rather middle-class complaints, but together with reproductive rights and the control of our own bodies, being shut out of education has always been the means by which the powerless are excluded from living the fullness of their own lives.

I find it difficult not to fall back into the language of the 1970s when I write about these things. Perhaps it is because the slogans remain as true to me today as they did then. Feminism has been the defining political principle of my own life. Without it I would have been a frustrated housewife, I dare say, dipping into the Valium bottle to tamp down my depression. The greatest prize I got in the lottery of life was freedom to make my own errors and my own sadnesses instead of the ones enforced upon me. Nothing else is worth a candle.

'We are either going to have
a future where women lead the way to make
peace with the Earth or we are not going
to have a human future at all'

Vandana Shiva

15
Nathalie Handal

For the Record

She walked into my room, said in a French accent with a hint of Arabic, 'There are two ways to be a woman: clever and clever.' I was ten years old. My Lebanese grandmother, who rode a bicycle in her youth when it was still considered a sin, her long braided blonde hair against the sun, didn't explain further. I jumped out of bed, ran to her and held her hand, nails painted with signature electric-crimson polish. She was smoking her cigarette, as she usually did, as if in a Greta Garbo movie, and looked at me, her piercing eyes telling me I should understand. If I didn't, I should figure it out.

A few years later, Anita, who looked after me, was by the outdoor water tap. Her dream was to educate herself, but like her mother she got pregnant at a young age and had to work in service – an option for many poor women in the Antilles – to support her daughter. The afternoon dimming the Caribbean light on her shoulders, she sat on a low bamboo chair, typical of the islands, a small, round bucket on the floor stationed steadily between her feet in pale blue rubber flip-flops. I sat beside her as she hummed a church song and washed white cloth in the red plastic bucket. I did not want to disturb her calm. But as I watched her lift two sides of the cloth, rub them together back and forth, return them to the water and start over as the foam from the Fab detergent thickened, I couldn't stop from asking, 'Why?' She smiled: 'It looks like life.' I didn't understand how a bucket of soapy cloth could look like life. Then she added in Creole, 'Little one, watch, understand the repetitions. Be clever. Now tell me one of your stories.'

Last year I found my friend Samia at the edge of her window in her stone house in Jerusalem. She said, 'A woman's quietness can disturb a man.' She leaned forward, almost falling before finding her balance again. My heart pounding, I asked her to stop. She looked at the stores below, the cars honking, the man selling *kaak*, and said, 'I keep returning to my head.' She recollected after reporting a story in Afghanistan: 'Nadia's son joined the Taliban. Her daughter wrote. Every evening, she would wake up in the middle of the night to write poems in the dark so as not to raise any suspicion of her audacity – a woman writing. When she finished, she would go to the window and like magic see her lines perfectly straight on every page. She hid them under the mattress. The day they found out her brother was killed, her father, in rage and in grief, shook his daughter's bed and the pages spread across the floor like a testament challenging fate. He beat his daughter to death. Nadia did not say anything to her husband, she knelt by her daughter's body, held her tight, went to the window where her daughter once read her verses, and fell.' Samia walked away from the edge. She wanted to feel what it was like to risk a life to write a poem. That thrill. That sudden impact to the heart. 'The problem,' she told me, 'is if women are equal to men, who is the world?'

The words 'be clever' came back to me. I didn't know at the time, but these women were telling me that being clever meant being brave. For my grandmother, the only path to consider was a woman's own. She advised me that I didn't need to explain to anyone, that my words would be in my actions. Anita expressed that it was my responsibility to define myself. My mind is my passion, the most important tale. From Samia, I learned that men wage war when they lack imagination, and that without the evolution of women, no society can evolve. Nadia's quietness was not silence but an assertion, *I will not lie any more*. Being women, it took courage for them to imagine.

Adrienne Rich said, 'The connections between and among women are the most feared, the most problematic, and the most potentially transforming force on the planet.' Months before Adrienne died, a mutual friend sent me an email saying, 'Adrienne said she'd love to hear from you.' She was one of the first supporters of my work. I took too long to write – I thought, I'll see her in Santa Cruz when I go in May. She died in March.

Driving away from the KUSP Central Coast Public Radio station where I was an in-studio guest, I thought of Adrienne who had lived close by. Her line 'Ask where you were' tells me what it's like to be a woman today. And yes, *for the record*, they were right: 'The song is higher than the struggle.'

16

Natalie Haynes

Sex, Feminism and the Ancient World

In 411 BCE Athens was in the golden age of her democracy. She had also been embroiled in a war with the southern Greek city-state of Sparta for twenty years. Athens was a mighty sea power, but Sparta had the greatest army the ancient world had ever seen. Neither city was strong enough to win the war; both were strong enough to inflict terrible damage on their opponents. The Athenians had been debilitated further with their disastrous expedition against Syracuse in Sicily a couple of years earlier.

But even as this military disaster played out, in Athens, in the city itself, culture and thought were thriving. Socrates was badgering people to define beauty and truth and piety. Sophocles and Euripides were writing some of the greatest tragedies anyone has ever produced. And the comic playwright Aristophanes staged *Lysistrata* for the first time. It's one of his greatest plays: a comic fantasy in which the women of Greece finally lose patience with their warmongering men.

Women, of course, had no political power in Athens. Sure, they might have influenced their husbands (Socrates once claimed he learned everything he knew about public speaking from Aspasia, the foreign-born wife of the great statesman Pericles, though it's hard to judge how serious he was), but they couldn't vote. Athens' great democracy was only for men, and citizen men at that; women, foreigners and slaves were not invited to join.

It's worth bearing all this in mind when you realize that within a hundred years of this democracy coming into being, Aristophanes – a comedian, but a conservative-minded one – was asking the question: what would happen if women got involved in politics? The answer is a happy one. The women have no political power, in the play as in reality, so they decide to get their own way by holding a sex strike. They will, quite literally, not make love till the men in their lives stop making war.

The play is bawdy and incredibly funny. The men all appear onstage wearing large, stick-on phalluses, the women are all nymphomaniacs, so resisting the lure of sex with a husband back from the war is genuine agony for these characters. Still, the women have sworn an oath, and they just manage to stick to it. It's worth it, because eventually the men agree to a truce, and all can fall into a long-overdue embrace. And of course, this joke could have been told in exactly the same way for well over two thousand years, until women got the vote, and the chance to hold political office.

And then, in 2011, Belgium entered the record books. It smashed the record, previously held by Iraq, for going for the longest period without a government, something it managed to do for 541 days. During the deadlock, a Belgian senator,

Marleen Temmerman, suggested that things might be more quickly resolved if the sexual partners of those who were failing to negotiate a deal went on a sex strike.

And at this point it's worth mentioning that, while this looks like the same joke as Aristophanes makes in the play, it has actually changed.

Aristophanes was a man with a vote, and a voice and a track record of making political jokes. He was writing about the relatively powerless from a position of relative power. Also when his heroine Lysistrata walks onstage and explains her plan to halt the war, she is being played (behind a mask) by a man. All the female characters in the play are men wearing masks.

If women were allowed in the audience for comedies (we don't know for sure that they were, comedy being a risqué business, at least if you do it right), they were laughing at something entirely alien: female characters written by men, performed by men, refusing to grant sexual favours to other men, also played by men. Even Germaine Greer might take a minute to unpick the politics of gender identity at work here.

But when Temmerman made the suggestion of a sex strike, it was no longer a joke a man makes about women – it had become a joke made by a woman who was holding elected office, about her fellow politicians and their spouses. It's still a joke about sex, in other words, but it's no longer one about gender. Temmerman is not just a politician, she is also an obstetrician-gynaecologist who works at the International Centre for Public Health. She won the *BMJ*'s Lifetime Achievement Award in 2010 for her work as a pioneer in women's health. And when a gynaecologist suggests a sex strike, it is rather different from a comedian doing so.

Temmerman had a more recent historical precedent available to her than Aristophanes: in Kenya, in 2009, women's groups had called for a sex strike to try and break a deadlock between the country's president and its prime minister. Temmerman described how these women had called for the first lady and the wife of the prime minister to join their sex strike, and how financial inducements were apparently offered to Kenyan prostitutes to try to compensate them for lost earnings if they joined in with the strike. 'The impact,' she admitted when she proposed the same tactic in Belgium, 'has never been scientifically proven. But within one week, there was a stable government.'

And that is why feminism and sex and jokes are fascinating, at least to me. From the very dawn of democracy, a man was wondering what it would be like to have women getting involved in politics. He writes a play about this idea which is so scabrous and funny that people are still performing it two-and-a-half millennia later. The idea behind that play is so interesting, quite aside from being funny, that people are still thinking about it, joking about it, seriously suggesting it, or putting it into practice now. And the joke behind that idea is so good that even as women have eventually acquired political clout, it still works.

'The first thing I do in the morning is brush
my teeth and sharpen my tongue'

Dorothy Parker

17
Sharon Haywood
Owning the F-word

I was always a feminist . . . I just didn't know it.

As a teen and a young woman, I would rattle off misinformed excuses for not owning feminism, and it doesn't seem to have changed much with up-and-coming generations. Take twenty-two-year-old Taylor Swift, internationally acclaimed pop-country singer, who when asked whether she was a feminist responded, 'I don't really think about things as guys versus girls. I never have. I was raised by parents who brought me up to think if you work as hard as guys, you can go far in life.' It wasn't until my thirties, when I left my provenance of Canada to explore other cultures, that I came to learn that feminism is not a battle of the sexes, and sometimes working hard simply isn't enough. It took moving to Argentina, where 15 per cent of cosmetic surgery patients are teenage girls seeking Botox injections, chin implants and lip fillers, for me to become a card-carrying feminist.

By the 1980s, just as I grew old enough to form my own

opinion, the backlash aimed at the second wave of feminism was firmly entrenched in popular culture. The media and entertainment industry did (and still do) a fine job of depicting feminists as militant, hairy and angry, strengthening the stereotype that no one I knew wanted to be associated with. I bought into the propaganda that feminists were man-hating, undesirable and humourless, adjectives I most certainly did not want attached to my name.

Although I recognized that many of my basic rights – voting, getting a credit card, attending university and having full reproductive autonomy – came courtesy of earlier generations of feminists, I couldn't relate to them. A combination of immaturity, widely accepted delegitimizing stereotypes and having never known a real-life feminist shaped my belief that the women's movement had finished its job. Even though my core values aligned with feminism, I fervently defended my beliefs in equality by tagging on the disclaimer, 'Yes, but I'm not a feminist,' lest I be ostracized from mainstream society. I rejected the F-word when I called out my friends on sexist jokes, when I maintained catcalling is sexual harassment and even when I defended my undergraduate thesis arguing the association between pornography and violence against women. The relationship between less obvious forms of oppression in my midst and the work of earlier feminists eluded me.

Argentina changed that. For almost a decade I have lived in a country whose leader, the second female president in the nation's history, insists she is 'feminine', not a 'feminist'. Argentina is the first Latin American country to legally institute gay marriage and afford basic rights to the transgender community, yet abortion remains illegal. Women occupy almost 40 per cent of the seats in the Senate, but the country holds one of the highest global rates of gender wage disparity. Buenos Aires is one of the most multicultural cities in South America, populated with a diverse range of body types, but roughly 30 per cent of women, only the smaller-framed ones, can find fashionable clothes in their size. Living in this land of dichotomies where the oppressed reality of women is magnified to the nth degree jolted me out of my feminism-shunning stance. I saw how Argentine women rely on feminists to advocate for the basic rights I was privileged to be born with, not unlike how previous generations of women in the developed world depended on pioneering feminists. As I connected the dots, I also came to the horrific realization that I had given mere lip service to the brave women before me. Viewing my own culture from an outside perspective under-scored the importance of owning the label in the fight against the subtle, and sometimes not-so-subtle, sexism still very present in the developed world.

When I finally had my light-bulb moment, or rather, was smacked over the head by the obvious, I craved community. Feminism in Buenos Aires is generally considered a four-letter word in everyday interactions, requiring feminists to seek out like minds via organizations dedicated to women's rights. Not yet feeling brave enough to step into the feminist fray, I sought refuge online – and found it. The virtual world of activism offered me a safe space to explore and expand my understand-ing of gender equity. It also inspired me to act. I immersed myself in social media, signed petitions, wrote essays and arti-cles and joined the AnyBody and Adios Barbie teams. As I realised what was possible with only my laptop, an internet con-nection and mutually supportive activists from around the world, I mustered the courage to become involved in feminist circles in Argentina and launch an Endangered Bodies chapter in Buenos Aires.

Since I've owned feminism, my life has changed for the better. It has heightened my sensitivity to the different experi-ences of all people as they intersect with various aspects of their identity. It's improved the quality of my personal relationships with others and myself. And it's affirmed that a small group of committed people can indeed effect positive change. That said, imagine what our world would look like if feminism wasn't restricted to the fringe.

Study after study has shown that feminist self-identity lends to greater collective action, thus increasing the likelihood of social change. From Argentina to Australia, the more of us who own feminism as part of who we are, the greater our odds of raising consciousness and dissolving the rhetoric that stands in the way of gender equity. Perhaps with more life experience, celebrity role models like Taylor Swift and other well-known self-proclaimed non-feminists – actress-director Drew Barrymore, singer-songwriter Björk and Yahoo! CEO Marissa Mayer, to name a few – will recognize that they too are in fact feminists, and pave a less-obstructed path for all women. Taking ownership of the label doesn't require abandoning the role of a stay-at-home mother, earning a doctorate in gender studies or founding a non-profit organization (and it certainly doesn't trigger overnight facial hair), but it does mean possessing and wielding our combined potential and power to achieve genuine equality.

Individually, it starts with the assertion, *Yes, I am a feminist.*

18
Lindsey Hilsum
Front Line

In the 1930s the wonderfully named American journalist Hubert Renfro Knickerbocker said: 'Whenever you see hundreds of thousands of sane people trying to get out of a place and a little bunch of madmen struggling to get in, you know the latter are newspapermen.'

Madwomen too. I met the *Sunday Times* foreign correspondent Marie Colvin in 1998. War had broken out between Ethiopia and Eritrea, and the little bunch was in Djibouti, eyeing up planes ferrying out aid workers and businesspeople from the Eritrean capital, Asmara. A pair of Ukrainian pilots agreed to turn round and take us in. Walking to the plane through the sweltering heat, we could see that they had rinsed out their shirts and hung them from the wings. As we taxied down the lumpy runway, the shirts blew away – our pilots were flying bare-chested. The aircraft lurched upwards and the TV gear that had been piled at the front gradually slid down the aisle. Convinced we were going to die, Marie and I laughed so much we nearly fell out of our seats.

Why do we do it? Partly for those moments of adventure and camaraderie; but Marie believed we could make a difference, that our stories might cause governments or people to act. For her, it was always about people, not weapons – she was more interested in telling the stories of those caught up in war than in analysing the strategies of generals.

'Covering a war means going to places torn by chaos, destruction, and death, and trying to bear witness,' she once wrote. 'It means trying to find the truth in a sandstorm of propaganda when armies, tribes or terrorists clash. And yes, it means taking risks.'

In the tradition of Martha Gellhorn, who got round the rules banning women reporters from the frontline in the Second World War by stowing away on a ship carrying nurses, Marie was glamorous as well as brave. She wore La Perla underwear beneath her flak jacket, and when she was home from assignment liked nothing more than to slither into a little black cocktail dress and throw a party. 'We've got to have a little femininity,' she said once, when someone pointed out she was wearing pink socks in Iraq. For her, being female was no impediment. When other journalists pulled out of East Timor in 1999, she and two Dutch female reporters stayed behind in the beseiged UN compound. Her editor asked why all the men had left. 'I don't know,' she said. 'I guess they don't make men like they used to.'

I suspect that Marie, like me, would say that it's the men in the newsroom, rather than in the countries where we report, that have caused us most grief. Twenty years ago, when I applied for a job as Egypt correspondent, one of the all-male interview board suggested that the job would be harder for me because of my gender. On the contrary, I said, it's harder for men. As a Western woman I am not excluded from meetings with male political leaders or generals – rather, I am treated as an honorary man. But in Muslim countries, traditional women will not talk to a man outside the family, so male reporters often cannot get women's stories. Of course you shouldn't discriminate against the other candidates, I said, but the fact is that a man can't do the job so well.

Needless to say, I didn't get the position; it went to a man who (my male boss helpfully pointed out) had the advantage of an Egyptian wife. But I think about that interview when I look back over my career. I watched the historic handshake between the Israeli Prime Minister, Yitzhak Rabin, and the Palestinian leader, Yasser Arafat, on TV with three generations of Palestinian women, in a tiny house in a refugee camp in Jordan. I doubt that a man would have been invited. In Afghanistan, my all-female team – including a woman camera operator, which is still quite unusual – got access to a project training young women as teachers. A cameraman would not have been allowed to film, and I doubt the girls would have talked to a male reporter about their aspirations in the way they talked to us.

I come across far more women reporting from the front lines now than when Marie and I started as foreign correspondents in the 1980s. On the whole, men and women run similar risks, but in 2011 several female journalists were sexually assaulted in Tahrir Square in Cairo as they covered the Arab Spring uprising. Lara Logan of CBS described how a mob of two hundred men raped her 'with their hands' in a terrifying attack as President Mubarak was overthrown. It could have been any of us – we were all in the square that night. In the face of real danger, we cannot pretend there is no problem; but it is not one that can be solved, as the French organization *Reporters Sans Frontières* suggested, by editors not sending female correspondents to Egypt. In such dangerous circumstances we have to work in mixed-sex groups, sometimes with security guards, minimize the time we spend in a dangerous place and on occasion hold back from going into crowds. We can only reduce, not eliminate, danger, and allow women to decide individually whether the risk is too great. Egyptian women face these dangers all the time – vigilante groups are now pouncing on harassers in the street because the police do nothing.

In February 2012 Marie was in the city of Homs as the neighbourhood of Baba Amr came under mortar attack by Syrian government forces. Her dispatch that Sunday described the 'Widow's Basement' where three hundred women and children sheltered as their neighbourhood was systematically destroyed. I spoke to her on Skype. 'Lindsey, this is the worst we have ever seen,' she said. I begged her to leave.

Shortly after dawn on 22 February, rockets started to fall on either side of the media centre where the small group of journalists in Homs were staying. The targeters were homing in. The shell that killed Marie also killed a young French photographer, Remi Ochlik. It did not discriminate by gender.

'Freedom is always the freedom
to think differently'

Rosa Luxemburg

19
Isabel Hilton

Empress Wu

Watching a TED talk the other day by a woman executive in Silicon Valley, I was struck by one neat formulation she produced: power correlates positively to likeability in men and negatively in women. It is not a new thought, but I was reminded of it as I watched the seven men who had reached China's ruling inner circle – the Standing Committee of the Politburo – march onstage. In their identical suits, red ties and implausibly dyed hair, they looked like contestants in a bizarre production of *China's Got Talent* choreographed by North Korea, but I am sure that none of the obligingly applauding audience thought the line-up unnatural. Men in power remains the order of things.

Public memory has not been kind to the handful of women who have held power in China's roughly three thousand years of recorded history. The neo-Confucian tradition insists that a woman who wields power is like a hen that crows. The two female Politburo members who might have made it to Standing Committee in 2012 have a lot to overturn.

The stock character in this narrative is a woman who rises on the back of her powerful husband, only to misuse her position. Bo Xilai's wife, the lawyer Gu Kailai, currently serving life for the alleged murder of the British citizen Neil Heywood, falls into this category, as does Jianq Qing, Mao's fourth wife, a former film actress who led the assault on traditional culture in the Cultural Revolution.

I met Jiang Qing in 1974, at a concert in the Great Hall of the People in Beijing. The excitement of the moment was that, after ten years of enforced puritanism and sartorial conformity in China – the baggy-blue-suit decade – Jiang Qing was wearing a dress, the only woman in China who could do so at the time without fear. It is hard to argue that she was the best example of female power: I suffered through countless classes in Shanghai, her local power base, as the teacher struggled to present Jiang's literary theory as anything other than dogmatic absurdity. Her persecution of artists and intellectuals was cruel and vindictive and she was part of a power group that wrecked countless lives. But when she fell, the public hatred of the Gang of Four was focused overwhelmingly on her. Scenes from her televised trial in 1980 show her contemptuous and unrepentant. She committed suicide in prison in 1991.

Jiang Qing's reputation was no worse than that of Cixi, the fearsome Empress Dowager of the closing years of the Qing Dynasty, who is chiefly remembered for maintaining her position by doing away with rival family members and spending the money allocated for a much-needed navy on a marble boat in the lake of her new Summer Palace. She, in turn, fares no worse than the Tang Dynasty's Empress, Wu Zetian (625–705 AD). Wu was the only woman ever to rule China as Empress in her own right, and characteristically she has gone down in history as an example of why women should never be allowed to take power. In fact, she ruled China rather more effectively and benignly than many men.

The Tang Dynasty (618–907 AD) was a great deal more appealing than most that preceded or followed it. Its rulers had ethnic ties to Central Asia and the dynasty they created was cosmopolitan, outward-looking and economically successful. Its open trade borders, and the success of the Silk Road, brought people from all over the medieval world to the streets of the capital, Chang'an (present-day Xi'an). It was the golden age of Chinese poetry and painting, and music and dance flourished. It was also a good time for women – it was pre-foot-binding, for one thing. In the Musée Guimet in Paris there is a fabulous group of Tang Dynasty ceramic figures that depicts a group of women playing polo. The horses are at full gallop, the women are riding astride, swinging their mallets, alive, fully in control and clearly having a wonderful time. It is exuberant, carefree and thrilling, an image of women's possibilities that would become unrecognizable in later Chinese history.

Wu was from a prominent family and at fourteen she was sent to be one of many concubines of the emperor Tai Zong. The Emperor died when Wu was twenty-seven, at which point, rather than spending the rest of her days as a Buddhist nun, as tradition dictated, she rather adroitly became first concubine, then wife and finally Empress to his son Gaozong. Five years later, when Gaozong had a stroke, Wu effectively ran the country, lasting until 705 when, old and ill, she was deposed. She kept her title of Empress and died at the end of that year, aged eighty.

It comes as no surprise that today her ruthlessness and cruelty are thought of as her defining characteristics. She has been accused of killing her own daughter to frame a rival, and of many executions and poisonings, the usual routes to medieval power for people without entitlement.

But even hostile contemporary historians gave her credit for running a brilliant administration, albeit with the help of a secret police force that she built. She embraced Buddhism as her state religion and invited scholars and artists to create some of the most magnificent pieces of religious art that China has ever produced. And, unlike some less sisterly women who got to the top, Wu saw improvements to the status of other women as a key factor in her own legitimacy.

She promoted her mother and other female relatives to important posts and had biographies of famous women written. She established public examinations as the official means of recruiting talent, and promoted scholars over soldiers in her administration. She was, early Chinese historians grudgingly admit, a brilliant judge of character: if her officials did a good job, they were rewarded with her approval. If they failed her, they could expect no mercy. She would clearly have made a terrific CEO.

Compare this to one of the most celebrated characters in Chinese history, Qin Shihuangdi (259–210 BCE), the first Emperor of the Qin Dynasty, much admired by Mao Zedong for what we might call his decisive politics and revered by today's regime as the founder of China. His ten-thousand-year Reich collapsed within three years of his death, and nobody disputes that he was a paranoid and cruel despot: he had more than four hundred scholars buried alive and another seven hundred stoned to death for having the temerity to hold views that did not coincide with his own, and tens of thousands of people died labouring on his monumental public works. Yet Qin Shihuangdi is remembered as a great ruler, while Empress Wu is a woman who forgot her place.

The examination system Wu promoted lasted for more than a thousand years. Sadly, in later centuries, the only role women played in the examination system was as seducers in the pseudonymous fiction of the late Ming Dynasty. In these stories, the young scholar hero, on his way to the capital to take his exams, is bewitched by a beautiful woman. In the morning, the enchantress has vanished and only the faintly rank smell that lingers on the bed alerts the young man, too late, to the fact that he has been fatally seduced by a fox fairy. I like to see the guiding spirit of Empress Wu in this sabotage of male ambition, her last revenge on a nation incapable of honouring her talents.

20

Rachel Holmes

Did Eleanor Marx Have a Telephone?

In 1898 a woman from London named Eleanor Marx had a late-morning bath, dressed in white, went to bed and killed herself. The two ounces of chloroform and one fluid dram of prussic acid, prescribed for poisoning a dog she didn't have, were sufficient to kill several humans.

Why didn't you call me?

I would have rushed to you, by train and omnibus, sprinted through the bare winter trees along Jews Walk. Been there, witness, not let you die alone. You should have called.

I get hard-to-get. But keeping me on hold for a hundred years? That's pushing the point. *Philosophers have hitherto interpreted the world. The point is to change it.* That's what your dad has impressed on his headstone at Highgate, where he rots in earthy embrace with your mother Jenny and Helen, the housekeeper. (Is there something we should know?)

In lean years you rolled discount tobacco and went hungry for weeks to pay for fresh garlands to crown the grave every anniversary. True to your materialist gospel of death, you, burned up, unburied, leave me no final resting place to visit.

Your ashes went missing for ages, by the way. Edward skipped your cremation for a football match. Promptly filed probate for your material remains, but never picked up what was left of you. No one was surprised.

Some unknown comrade did make the effort to collect your stardust from Croydon though. Epochs later, during a Cold War police raid on the headquarters of the British Communist Party, your urn toppled from a shelf, caught just before it smashed amid overturned desks and censored papers. A letter inside identifies these as the ashes of the daughter of socialism.

Eleanor Marx. Daddy's little girl. The son he wished survived. Indulged youngest, multilingual, precocious *garçon manqué*. Inheritor of the family trade: changing the world. Father – most famous philosopher of the modern age. Mother? Sorry to say that despite everything you wrote in *The Woman Question* (1886), she's been given a pasting. You wouldn't recognize your own mother in the sour clichés of prudish, complaining snobbery peddled by posterity so far.

Your *mutti*, Jenny von Westphalen, youth activist and scholar, the girl who pinned the revolutionary tricolour in her hair, loved parties and dancing, inspired the members of Young Germany with luminous speeches, whose intellect and bold radicalism the young Karl gazed up at in admiration. Red Jenny, the brilliant woman who pawned her life to hold your father and family together for half a century. Always with her, shoulder to shoulder, your second mother Helen, history's housekeeper. But that's another story.

Put the women who made you back into your life and we begin to make sense of it. *Cherchez la femme*, as you used to say, amused by the inconstancy of men.

'Tussy *is* me,' said Papa portentously; your mother rolled her eyes and briskly retorted, 'Tussy is political from top to toe.' No one can remember the time before your nickname was Tussy. To rhyme, your parents said, with 'pussy', not 'fussy'. Cats you adored; fussy you weren't. Tussy = 2C: MC Victorian socialist feminist internationalist revolutionary rapper spinning discs for radical overthrow of patriarchal capitalism. 2C or not 2C, that is the question; Shakespeare and bad puns, you loved both equally.

Suicide at forty-three. Tipping a phial of prussic acid down your throat is not a call for help. Deathly dose administered by your hand, alone. Or was it? You go first, Edward said, I'll follow later. Unilateral Suicide Pact? Now there's a contradiction and USP for you to unpick, Ms Marxist. That's Edward all over.

Why didn't you call?

'Operator here, collect call waiting for Dr Holmes, twenty-first century, from Ms Marx in 1898, will you accept the charges?'

'Rachel?'

'Eleanor! Hey, this is a party line – others listening in.'

'Call me Tussy. Good to talk finally, but I don't hold with party lines, as you know.'

'Thanks. I call you every day. Keep getting your old message.'

Hi, you've reached the voicemail of Eleanor Marx, feminist, socialist, activist, trade unionist, organizer, orator, teacher, economist, political theorist, social philosopher, writer, translator, historian, caregiver to my parents and nephews, dupe of a scoundrel husband, and bad amateur actress. I'm quite busy changing the world right now, so please leave a message and I'll get back to you as soon as I've succeeded.

'I really must update that message. All that *Sturm und Drang* feminism and struggle must be defunct by now. So, you're writing my life, how's it going?'

'Frankly, it would be a bit easier if you'd done less. Operated on fewer levels. You know, history man version: win big war, drink whisky, hide black dog, let wife and women handle the children and Life: The Backstory. Right now you're living a lifetime in a year. I know you won't slow down, you never did.'

'Enough already! Sounds exhausting, even to the dead. Good thing I topped myself early, imagine the challenge if I'd scored a century.'

'Wish you had. You would have been able to see girls go to school, young women go to university, control our reproduction, vote, enter public office, fly planes, become Olympians, discover DNA and pulsar stars and – talking of centuries – we've got a national first eleven now.'

'How many British women prime ministers so far?'

'Just the one.'

But Tussy's call is only in my head, and these, imaginary lines.

By the late 1890s several of her Sydenham neighbours had telephones. Eleanor, early adopter of the typewriter, enthusiast for all new technology, couldn't afford a phone. I would have come if you'd called me. But I wouldn't have be able to save you. Not then, not now. You'd win the argument, as you always did. Give me, you'd say, one good reason why women are not free and equal to men in all things. 'And first, a general idea that has to do with all women. The life of woman does not coincide with that of man. Their lives do not intersect; in many cases do not even touch.' You wrote that in 1886. I can't tell you that it's no longer true.

We've made progress – though it's far from as international as you'd wish. The revolution has halted but the wheels are still turning. I have daily freedoms you could only dream of, and many other things your work delivered. Thank you, sister outrider. But there's still far to go. We don't need to re-reinvent the wheel, we need to harness an atomic rocket to it. Thank you for teaching me the long view of history.

'We must all make do with the
rags of love we find flapping on the
scarecrow of humanity'

Angela Carter

Posy Simmonds

21

Siri Hustvedt

Underground Sexism: What Was That You Just Said?

As a white, educated, American woman from a middle-class family, I have not suffered the horrors of overt, brutal misogyny. I was never subjected to genital mutilation or sold to a man as his wife or sex slave. No one told me I couldn't go to school, learn to drive, own property or stride down a city street alone. I have the right to vote, and I make my own living as a writer. And yet, despite my advantages over so many women in the world, I am keenly aware that even among supposedly enlightened, left-leaning, right-thinking men and women, sexism is a widespread, corrosive presence that distorts all of us, even when it is not malicious or even conscious.

I am a woman writer married to a man writer (note that the latter sounds bizarre but the former doesn't), and I have often been thrown into situations that have forced me to ask whether I am encountering sexism (either conscious or unconscious) or something else. Was the male journalist who suggested that my husband had written my first novel a sexist, or was he just goading me because I was married to a well-known writer? What about the grand old man of French publishing who had read my third novel and with a magisterial wave of his hand, said, 'You should keep writing'? *Did he honestly think he had a say in whether I wrote or not?* When men repeatedly tell me that they do not read fiction but their wives do, and they'd like me to sign my book to their spouses, what does their resistance to fiction signify? Do they include Homer, Dante and Shakespeare in the ban? Or do they mean they don't read female writers like me?

Unconscious bias isn't always easy to detect or analyse. In her book *Why So Slow?: The Advancement of Women*, the linguist and psychologist Virginia Valian discusses what she calls 'implicit gender schemas', unconscious ideas about masculinity and femininity that infect our perceptions and which tend to overrate the achievements of men and underrate those of women. I call this 'the masculine enhancement effect'. Research has shown that women in positions of power are routinely evaluated less highly than their male counterparts, even when there is no difference in performance. A 2004 study, 'Penalties for Success: Reactions to Women Who Succeed at Male Gender-Typed Tasks' (Heilman et al.), tells the story in its title. A 2008 study found that when academic papers were subject to double-blind peer review – neither the author nor the reviewer was identified – the number of female first-authored papers accepted increased significantly. A 2001 study by Laurie Rudman and Peter Glick concluded with these words: 'The prescription for female niceness is an implicit belief that penalizes women unless they temper their agency with niceness.' In order to be accepted women must compensate for their ambition and strength by being nice. Men don't have to be nearly as nice as women.

I do not believe women are inherently nicer than men. They

learn that niceness brings rewards and that naked ambition is often punished. Once mastered, all learning becomes unconscious and automatic, relegated to what scientists now call 'the cognitive unconscious'. Consciousness, it seems, is parsimonious, reserved for dealing not with what is routine and predictable in our lives, but with what is novel and unpredictable. Perception is by its very nature biased, a form of typecasting. More often than not, we see what we expect to see.

We, all of us, women and men, encode masculinity and femininity in implicit metaphorical schemas that divide the world in half. Science and mathematics are hard, rational, real, serious and masculine. Literature and art are soft, irrational, unreal, frivolous and feminine. In a paper advising teachers on methods that will encourage boys to read, I came across the following sentence: 'Boys often express distaste for reading as a passive, even feminine activity.' Presumably, understanding and manipulating numbers doesn't carry the same stigma. Since both numbers and letters are abstract signs, *genderless representations*, the prejudice against reading is nothing short of stupefying until one realizes that the bias is associative. Anything that becomes associated with girls and women loses status, whether it is a profession, a book, a movie or a disease.

A woman doing science is 'masculinized' by her choice of work. A male novelist, on the other hand, is 'feminized' by his job, and yet whatever he writes is made more serious by his male anatomy. A woman novelist is in double trouble as a woman who writes imaginary stories. Because I write fiction and non-fiction and have an abiding interest in neurobiology and philosophy (still mostly male disciplines), I embody the masculine/feminine, serious/not-so-serious, hard/soft divide in my own work. When I publish a paper in a science journal, I find myself on male terrain, but when I publish a novel, I stay squarely in female territory. Of course, this gendered geography is mostly hidden underground – unknown, unseen and un-articulated. Unconscious biases hurt women, but they also hurt men. If it is actually true that there are boys who think reading is for girls, heaven help us. I am sorry for men who feel emasculated by reading novels and doubly emasculated if the novel's author is a woman. Not only are they the victims of irrational prejudice, they deprive themselves of crucial knowledge about the world.

The good news is that unconscious patterns of perception and behaviour can be *made conscious*. Contemporary science confirms that our attitudes are shaped by implicit influences, but also that attention plays a role in reflective consciousness and judgement. Freud argued that once a neurotic becomes aware of his repetitive and injurious behaviours, he is in a position to change them. As feminists, it is our job to call attention to our cultural neuroses about masculinity and femininity. Sometimes it pays to be nice, but not always. I have discovered that the swift, acerbic retort can do wonders.

'The male desire to rule is the primary,
if not the only, stumbling block to women's
enlightenment. They are extremely suspicious
of women's emancipation.
Why? The same old fear: "Lest they
become like us"'

Kamini Roy

22
Jude Kelly
Unsuitable Behaviour

Today I went to see Gillingham FC (the Gills) play Morecombe (the Shrimpers) in the Football League Division Two. It was a trip down Memory Lane for my recently acquired bloke. He was brought up in the Medway Towns and hadn't been to the ground since he was a little boy – and he asked me along. And though I have minimal interest in football and probably a million more productive things to do on a Saturday afternoon, I thought, Why not?

So it's half-time in Gillingham, we're one goal up and on to the pitch run the little boy mascots, the junior team of boys (plus one girl) and twelve young female cheerleaders with bare midriffs and pom-poms. These hard-working teenage girls give a convincing show of synchronized sexual dance moves. I contemplate the issue of role models. We're a crowd of five thousand and we've just spent forty-five minutes lionizing and encouraging a group of young men to give us their all. No matter how slick their act, these young women can only get marginalized under the heading 'decorative crumpet'.

Most of the spectators leave to get refreshments. As I'm buying my atmospheric Bovril I spot a leaflet asking me to sponsor Gillingham Ladies for just £25 per season. 'Who are they and when do they play?' I ask the young woman serving me. 'I'm one,' she says, and goes on to explain that despite not being allowed to learn the sport at school she now plays every week in what is Kent's number-one women's football team. She tells me that they can't afford to play on Gillingham's own ground – too expensive – and they don't get help with the costs of stewards either, so they play their matches in comparative anonymity elsewhere.

So I'm back home on the internet, reading the following:

A Brief History of Women's Football

1895: The first women's football match North v. South. 7–1

1920: The first women's international game. Preston-based Dick, Kerr's Ladies beat a French XI 2–1. Attendance 25,000.

1920: The biggest crowd ever to date for a women's game. On Boxing Day 53,000 watch Dick, Kerr's Ladies beat St Helen's Ladies 4–0.

1921: The FA bans women from playing on a Football League ground: 'The game of football is quite unsuitable for females and ought not to be encouraged.'

1971: The FA council lifts the ban that forbade women from playing on the grounds of affiliated clubs.

2002: The FA announces that football has become the top participational sport for women and girls.

I consider the edict 'The game of football is quite unsuitable for females' – despite an enviable crowd of 53,000 presumably

in disagreement. It's Taliban-like in its own way. And I'm thinking what a deathly clamp the phrase 'unsuitable' has placed on
girls and women over the millennia. What makes pom-poms
and hair extensions suitable and muddy boots and goalie gloves
not? What makes baking bread and the cultivation of roses
suitable but erotic novels or women archbishops not? And
vice versa?

If we are really to liberate ourselves from the inhibitions
surrounding the 'unsuitable for females' attack, then we need
always to ensure that feminism offers true support to female
freedom and doesn't imply a theology of puritan intent.

I'm not sure what I think of boxing but I love the passion of
gold medallist Nicola Adams, which got her where she is in
surely the most macho of environments. I fell about laughing
when I heard that one world-famous maestro thinks it 'unsuitable' for a woman to conduct Verdi's *Otello*. But I also get cross
when women tell other women what's appropriate.

I've been a feminist for all my adult life. I've got form. But
that doesn't stop me sometimes wanting to paint my toenails an
unnatural colour or be stroked, cosseted and cradled like a helpless heroine. Sometimes. At other times I want to – and do –
run a major arts institution, direct plays, give speeches and generally try to ensure that nothing, not governments, nor old boys'
networks, not religious superstitions or society's norms, acts as
an impediment to my potential. But if I want it all – and why
not? – apparent inconsistencies and contradictions are inevitable.

I'm not a walking ideology and my moods and needs are
many and various. I notice my paramour – the nearest to an
alpha male I've ever walked out with – is totally relaxed about
striding the world like a Colossus yet close to tears when he finds
he's forgotten to pack his lucky underpants for a forthcoming
flight. He can command respect for his professional knowledge
and also crawl around the floor making encouraging noises at his

model railway. He can turn on the full testosterone and yet needs to be fed tomato soup from a spoon when he's feeling poorly.

So why can't I give myself full permission to have just as much scope to play around with the child/adult, girl/woman spectrum without worrying about looking strong or weak? Well, I think it's harder, much harder for women. I know that public and private judgement of our behaviour is harsher and more censorious and that too much evidence of fun and frivolity can serve to confirm our unsuitability for 'high office'. I know that other women can be the sternest members of the jury when we stand trial for lapses in perfection. But I'm convinced that feminism needs to be a big, bold, baggy over-coat that can accommodate each fully rounded female, with all her huge ambitions and cuddly toys. Shouldn't feminism be like a great partner – enjoying you for all that you are and can be?

Take this Saturday afternoon: I might worry that my girly compliance in going along with him and 'his' choice and 'his' environment and 'his' hobby was 'unsuitable'. But as my expected life gets shorter I've come to realize that there are better things to worry about than those elements of any ideology that, while supposed to be liberating, are at times in danger of constraining. And now I'm greeting romance like an old returning friend – and I don't let it bother my pretty little head.

Bring on wanton bad behaviour if the mood takes me. But in the spirit of equality, progress and symbolism, and because it's fun, me and my chap will be attending the next Gillingham Ladies home fixture to lionize them, to cheer them on.

And hopefully the pom-pom girls will be there too, strutting their stuff.

23
Liz Kelly

Changing it Up: Sexual Violence Three Decades On

The last few months have been remarkable for the sustained national and international debates on sexual violence. Two high-profile cases – Julian Assange and Jimmy Savile – garnered most attention, but as I write the Republican candidates in the US elections, who became notorious for their references to 'legitimate rape' and that conception following rape should be considered a 'gift from God', lost their seats. These powerful white men exercised not just feminists, but the left, the media and, perhaps most significantly in terms of feminist activism in the twenty-first century, social media. At issue has been what counts as violence/abuse, entitlement, impunity and complicity. This piece reflects on this moment to explore what gains have been made in understanding and responding to sexual violence since I became a feminist in the early 1970s, and the challenges we still face.

My name appears on an archived piece of paper – the argument for the deeply contested seventh demand of the British Women's Liberation Movement (WLM), on violence against women. For four decades I have been campaigning, writing, researching on this issue. For the record, and as a reference point for what follows, the seventh demand was: *Freedom for all women from intimidation by the threat or use of male violence. An end to the laws, assumptions and institutions which perpetuate male dominance and men's aggression towards women.*

In thinking about this piece, I tried to remember just why this statement was considered so divisive in the late 1970s: few would contest its content today; even the UN adopted a similar policy in the 1990s. Violence against women was a faultline in the many acrimonious debates between socialist and radical feminists in the 1970s, yet at the local level the reality was always more complex. Feminists of all shades established refuges and rape crisis centres in small towns and cities, like Norwich, where I discovered the WLM. It is easy to forget how much and how little we knew in the 1970s about the range and extent of violence. Initially we knew about ourselves – mainly white British, young and educated[1] – and our encounters with intimate intrusions, followed by the stories that the first women to seek safety and support shared with us. It would not be until the 1980s that prevalence research established just how common abuse was in most women's and children's lives.

The internal contestation in the first decade can be contrasted to the three that followed. Violence has been one of the issues through which feminists have created coalitions across contexts and continents: together we have taken it from margin to centre in public policy and international law. In many ways the shades of our feminism became less important than the issue we chose to focus on; on the other hand, as an argumentative movement debate, challenging exclusions and old and new orthodoxies have continued, taking many of us to new levels of complexity in our theory and practice.

Julian Assange: a question of entitlement and consent

Julian Assange came to public attention with the founding of Wikileaks, offering a safe online platform for leaked documents that expose governmental and corporate corruption, dishonesty and human-rights abuses. He achieved global recognition during 2010 when tens of thousands of documents relating to the wars in Afghanistan and Iraq were published by Wikileaks. Assange is a powerful anti-establishment figure, feted by parts of the left and human-rights defenders; he has a type of hero/celebrity status for so audaciously challenging the hegemony of the US. In 2010 he was also questioned by police in Sweden with respect to accusations of sexual assault, garnering him a different notoriety, sparking intense and acrimonious debates about sexual-offences law and the current stand-off between himself and the UK and Swedish governments. For those wishing to understand the events that followed I commend the forensic legal blogging by David Allen Green.[2]

What has been missed in the sound and fury is that sexual-offences law in many jurisdictions – and Sweden was actually a rather late joiner[3] – has shifted profoundly to accommodate the feminist, and now human-rights, principle of bodily and sexual integrity: a basic philosophical principle which feminism of many shades draws on, not just in relation to violence but also reproductive rights. At issue here is what counts as rape/sexual assault in law and life, and on the other side what does consensual sex look like – is it sought and is it given? A number of Left men, most notably Tony Benn[4] and George Galloway, have revealed the extent to which male MPs and sections of the Left have failed to follow this revolution in sexual politics. The responses of the Swedish health system, police and prosecutors and the courts in England suggest that feminists have had some impact on institutions, although both jurisdictions have seen the conviction rate for rape fall over two decades.[5]

Jimmy Savile: invisible in plain sight[6]

In perhaps the biggest crisis relating to the sexual abuse of children since the 1990s, the story about Jimmy Savile continues to unfold, revealing a man who was able to orchestrate a regime of abuse for over four decades, parading his impunity within and across institutions and to all those he abused. Here incredulity focuses on the licence he was afforded: unchecked sexual abuse has rocked the BBC, a quintessential British institution, and raised questions about two hospitals and a school for girls. That so many knew, or suspected, that his behaviour was problematic has led to questions about complicity and how the power of celebrity status can legitimize what in other contexts would be recognized as abuse. At the same time, the Savile case broke a dam of voices seeking to name their persecutors, and finding more belief and validation than has been evident in public discourse for some years. I would argue that this remains the case, despite the shift by some to all-too-familiar tropes of 'witch hunts' and 'moral panic' in mid-November 2012.

What has been lost are the early interventions by female broadcasters, beginning with Liz Kershaw talking about her experiences of sexual harassment and the pervading sexist culture in the BBC, which she connected to what it was that made it possible for Savile to be invisible in plain sight. Unsurprisingly, many male commentators contested this, paving the way for the weasel word 'paedophile' to dominate public discourse.

Changing it up

Yet again sexual violence sits at the heart of a crisis that rocks institutions. I am left wondering whether we have made more change than we recognize. Have there ever been more feminist and survivor voices – in the mainstream media and social media – refusing to be belittled or silenced?

Notes

1 That so many of us had been to – or were at – university did not make us middle class; many of us were the first in our families to do so.
2 www.newstatesman.com/blogs/david-allen-green/...assange
3 www.cwasu.org/filedown.asp?file=different_systems_03_web...
4 He subsequently changed his position following a challenge from students at Goldsmiths' College.
5 See note 2.
6 This is a play on a statement by Paul Gambaccini, who on *Panorama*, said Savile 'hid in plain sight. He said things that gave the game away, but nobody put two and two together'.

'As all advocates of feminist politics
know . . . most people learn about feminism
from patriarchal mass media'

bell hooks

24

Helena Kennedy QC

Eve Was Framed!

I have called myself a feminist since I was twenty. I was a child of the Red Clydeside and had been brought up in a working-class Glasgow family: people around me were canny about political reality. I was clued up about traditional class politics and had a strong sense of the power relations in society. When the Women's Movement started to make waves in the early 1970s, it gave me a new lens through which to see the world. Patriarchy was yet another force that constrained women's lives.

Even in communities where men got a rough deal and no straws were very long, women got the shortest straw. Yet I would bristle when I went to meetings in which middle-class women would hold forth on the male conspiracy, because I knew that the lives of working-class men were not great either. For me, feminism was never separated from my holistic view about the need for social reform across the board to create a more equal society. I had had a wonderful, loving father so I refused to characterize men as the enemy, and I had had a feisty mother who bowed to no one, so I hated depictions of women as victims. My feminism simply meshed into my established political framework, deepening my understanding of how societies worked.

Where feminism was different was that it connected politics to sex. The personal really was political. The arrival of the Pill in the previous decade had radically changed women's ability to control their fertility. Abortion legislation had been passed, ending the horrors of back-street abortion. Sexual liberation was the by-word. The old fears of getting pregnant could be taken out of sexual relations and sex was no longer coupled to marriage. The changes this brought to women's lives were immeasurable. Combined with a huge expansion of educational opportunities, it meant women could really make choices about how they lived. Dependency was no longer built into their place in the scheme of things. Relationships between men and women were being renegotiated.

Sexual politics was complicated for me. I had been brought up in a staunch Catholic family. But just by listening to conversations around my mother's kitchen table, I had grown embattled with the Church's teaching. Women in wretched marriages were told by priests that it was their duty to remain with abusive husbands. Abandoned women were vilified and denied Communion if they took up with another man. Girls of sixteen were forced to marry if they got pregnant. Families rejected daughters who wed Protestants. And on top of all that, celibate priests advised women on how to use the rhythm method of contraception to avoid pregnancy, a form of Russian roulette that tied women to large families and the kitchen sink. Knowledge of even that dicey form of birth control had been kept from women of my mother's generation, who just took their chances. Yet, despite all that, I still clung to the deep belief that sex was best if inextricably linked to love, so I trod a cautious path through the new seventies thickets. Recently, a feminist friend depicted me as a puny serial monogamist, which is true, but I have never found it disappointing.

My other departure from feminist semi-orthodoxy was that I maintained a visceral pleasure in dressing up. I loved lipstick and mascara, high heels and push-up bras, nail polish and scent. No political movement was going to inhibit my desire to make life glamorous, or my sensuous enjoyment of things that felt good, even if produced by corporate capitalism. Contradictions were the stuff of life. So I took the learning of feminism on board, but resisted the earnestness and puritanism that seemed too often to be its travelling companions. Dungarees were never part of my wardrobe. However, I refused to be cowed away from the word 'feminist' by the press depictions of feminists as miserabilists who hated men and fun. I have always loved both. I claimed the title 'feminist' as a proclamation and as an act of dissent.

It was practising in the courts that really drove home the lessons of feminism for me. The pain of my clients gave me my deepest lessons in oppression and inequality – cases of rape, sexual abuse, domestic violence, sexual harassment, discrimination in employment, discrimination in divorce settlements, discrimination on the grounds of sexuality, unequal pay, stalking, murder ... The rounds of misery, the strange acceptance of beatings because women became psychologically frozen. Feminism gave me a light to shine into dark corners of the law.

It was not so much that law was a conspiracy of men in long wigs, but that it was a product of male experience. It dealt with the world from a male perspective, because law was made by men – as judges, as legislators in Parliament, as legal commentators in the academic world. They ran it, controlled it, determined its content. Women were absent. And the tiny numbers of

women who had trickled into senior legal roles had learned to see
the world in the same way as their male tutors.

By the day, it was becoming clear to me as a young practi-
tioner that the problem was not just the attitudes of men on the
Bench and in the legal profession, which were bad enough; it
was that these had been translated into gendered law. Law itself
sustained inequality and prevented women securing justice. In
sexual offences, corroboration was required: there were judgements where judges actually said that the reason for the rule
was that women were inclined to invent sexual violation. The
law of evidence confined itself to the facts of the case in hand
and this circumscription often prevented the background of
a case becoming clear; for example, a long history of domestic
violence. The definitions of crimes or defences sometimes
worked against women: take 'provocation', where there had
to be proof that a defendant immediately snapped in the face
of provocation, and was no longer 'master of his own mind'.
Women, on the other hand, were more likely to respond to
sustained provocation, like frayed knicker elastic eventually
giving out in despair.

Women accused of crime are much fewer in number than
men, but they face a dual burden, as though they have somehow
offended against more than the criminal law and have failed society's standards of good womanhood. Battling against a system
entrenched in sexual double standards, which tested women on
a very different basis from men, stereotyping them into 'good'
and 'bad' because of their sexual conduct or capacity as wives or
mothers; challenging excruciating gender myths – this was hard
work.

Since the 1990s there have been great advances: women in
increasing numbers have entered the law and occupy senior
positions on the Bench. They may eschew the word 'feminist',
but equality is in their bloodstream. Men in the profession are

also now more sentient to the ways the system discriminates on gender lines. Yet the idea that we live in a post-feminist era, where women and men are now equal, is risible. Spend a few days in the courts and reality will hit home – sex trafficking, violence, stalking, rape, honour killing, the murder of children to punish their mothers. The cases will chill you to the bone.

Every time there is a new outpouring about women wanting to return to the hearth or women who just love being prostitutes or women who adore sexual submission, I turn the page. Of course women want more time for the people they love; of course women can become reconciled to selling sex as a livelihood; and of course women have all kinds of sexual fantasies. But to extrapolate anything meaningful from those truths is time-wasting. Our lives are complex. We are all products of much experience and many factors. What all women deserve is to be able to choose freely the lives they want to lead, free of oppression and exploitation, filled with opportunity to be who they want to be. It is *all* about human rights.

'In passing, also, I would
like to say that the first time Adam had a
chance, he laid the blame on a woman'

Nancy Astor

25
Kathy Lette
It's Still a Man's World

God, apparently as a prank, devised two sexes and called them 'opposite'. (Ah, if only there were a third sex available to us.) The sex war has raged since the dawn of humanity. Surely it's time we called a truce ... starting with men negotiating their terms of surrender. Now that women are economically independent and can impregnate ourselves, if only our vibrators could light the barbie and kill the spider in the bathtub, would we need men at all? There is much talk about the future being female, as catalogued in Hanna Rosin's bestseller *The End of Men: And the Rise of Women*. Women, the American writer points out, now hold half of the nation's jobs and in a third of families they are the main breadwinner. In the US, for every two men who receive a BA, three women will achieve the same.

And yet, misogynists, sexists – whatever you want to call those who don't treat women as equals – prove that dinosaurs still roam the earth. Worse, one hundred years since Emmeline Pankhurst chained herself to the railings of the British Prime Minister's house, women still don't have equal pay (we're getting 85 pence in the pound; in the US, it's about 75 cents in the dollar). We're also concussed from hitting our heads on the glass ceiling. Plus we're expected to Windolene it while we're up there (probably for £1.50 less than a man would be paid for doing the exact same task). What's more, even though females make up just under half of the workforce, we're still doing 99 per cent of all childcare and housework. The have-it-all Superwoman has turned into the do-it-all drudge.

A report published by British think-tank Demos reveals that women are being held down by a 'second glass ceiling' at home. Forty-four per cent of women interviewed said that they would take the day off work if their child was unexpectedly ill and couldn't go to school, but only 3 per cent said their husbands would do the same. Which could partly explain why only 3 per cent of FTSE 100 jobs are held by women. Many husbands seem to think that a woman's wedding vows read: 'To love, *hoover* and obey'.

Having raised two children, I'm convinced that the Dunkirk evacuation would be easier to organize than a working mother getting her kids up and out of the house in the mornings. My husband maintains he'd like to help more, only he can't multi-task. This is a biological cop-out; I doubt that any man would have trouble multi-tasking at, say, an orgy.

Then there's our representation in the media. When Australian Prime Minister Julia Gillard used the opposition leader Tony Abbott's testicles as maracas in her 'smack-down', it made global headlines. In Britain, France and the US she was praised for the most outspoken attack on sexism in political history. (The *Sydney Morning Herald*, following the release of a new *Herald*/Nielsen poll, reported a 5 per cent jump in Gillard's approval rating after the furore.) Yet much of the mainstream Australian media wrote off her speech as a disaster – something Lenore Taylor from the *SMH* put down to the male dominance of newspapers. According to Women in Journalism's analysis of nine national newspapers in the UK, sexist, humiliating stereotypes of women and male bylines dominate the front pages; during the past month, male journalists wrote 78 per cent of all front-page articles and men accounted for 84 per cent of those mentioned or quoted in lead pieces.

The only females to be regularly pictured in most newspapers are the Duchess of Cambridge and Pippa Middleton, who are little more than human handbags draped attractively over the arms of important men. When powerful women are featured, the images are often unflattering. There are few pictures in which women look businesslike; whereas men featured in newspapers wear suits and sports gear and are shown as active participants, women are sexualized objects, who are naked or nearly naked.

In other words, it's still a man's world.

Still, there's no doubt that feminism has improved things. When I was young, women climbed the career ladder lad by lad and wrong by wrong. Aged twenty-two, I went for a job interview at a major Australian television station. Four male executives sat across the desk from me. The most high-ranking of them slapped a $10 note on the table. 'I bet I can make your tits move without touching them,' he bragged. I shrugged, a little bewildered. He then lunged forward, mauled my breasts and shoved the money at me, guffawing, 'You won.' As the men smacked their thighs with matey mirth, I slapped $20 on the table and announced, 'I bet you twenty bucks I can make your balls move without touching them,' and kicked the executive who'd manhandled me hard between the legs. Yes, I got the job, but what an initiation.

According to websites such as the Everyday Sexism Project (everydaysexism.com), where women exchange examples of sexist remarks, chauvinism in the workplace is still rife.

So what are my survival tips for working women?

First off, if your boss comes on to you, I suggest you use a woman's most lethal weapon and shoot from the lip. Simply point at his appendage and say, 'What do you want me to do, *floss*?' Or enquire if he knows why men like intelligent women. Because opposites attract.

Even though women are brought up to be polite, sometimes we need to think like a bloke. The average man keeps fit by doing step aerobics off his own ego. So be confident and assertive. If a man tells sexist jokes to embarrass or unnerve you, fight back. Ask him if he knows why 'dumb blonde' jokes are always one-liners? So that men will understand them. Or perhaps enquire if he's heard about the miracle baby? It was born with a penis *and* a brain. If you're in banking, try asking if he knows the difference between government bonds and blokes. Government bonds mature. If a man ever refers to you as a 'cow' or a 'silly moo', just point out sweetly that the reason men can't get mad cow disease is because they're pigs. And if he retorts that women can't tell jokes, simply reply: 'That's because we work for them.'

Working mothers juggle so much we could be in the Moscow State Circus. But don't try to be perfect. Perfect mums only exist in American sitcoms. Just remember that a 'balanced meal' is whatever stays on the spoon *en route* to a baby's mouth. And 'controlled crying' is the art of not shattering into tears when your toddler accidentally wipes Vegemite all over your new designer suit.

And if you want to be in a top FTSE 100 job, I would also suggest you marry a man who likes to shop and mop. A beta bloke will adore you, won't bore you and will do all your chores for you – a 'wife', in other words.

Men often get pay rises because they ask. Don't be shy about highlighting your superior qualities. When it's promotion time, remind the boss how much time men waste. Not only is 'hypochondria' Greek for man (any man who says he's not a hypochondriac, that's the only disease he *doesn't* have) but they also think sitting on the toilet is a leisure activity.

And most important of all, be helpful to female colleagues. Women are each other's human Wonderbras: uplifting, supportive, making each other look bigger and better. And finally, remember that any woman who calls herself a 'post-feminist' has kept her Wonderbra and burned her brains, because we still have a long way to go.

'The worst mistake of a woman
is to go to the kitchen, because then
she never gets out of there'

Shakira

Posy Simmonds

26

Kate Mosse

Not the Only Fruit

Described as entrepreneurial, provocative, brilliant, brainy, sassy, energetic, groovy and – oh dear – sexist, retrogressive ... the Women's Prize for Fiction set out to do things differently. After seventeen years sponsored by Orange, in 2013 the prize comes of age and moves into a new stage – a good time to reflect on why and how it launched, what it's achieved and what's changed.

Here's how it happened. After an all-male Booker Prize short-list in 1991, a group of women and men in the trade (publishers, journalists, booksellers, agents, writers, librarians) gathered in a north London flat on a January night in 1992. Interviewers always say to me about that initial gathering, 'Surely you must have been "angry"?' Each time, the same answer: No, not angry. Thoughtful.

The spirit of that meeting was one of enquiry, of reflection, of question. Did it matter that there were no women on the Booker list (especially since the novels that had made it through were so strong)? Did it matter that the judges appeared not to have noticed? How might the press have reacted if it had been an all-female list instead? Would it have been seen as a political act, the worst kind of equal opportunity?

An evening of debate, red wine and enthusiasm resulted in consensus and a plan. The group acknowledged the need for accurate data – and we spent the next few years gathering that together – but our gut instincts turned out to be pretty accurate: that, give or take, some 60 per cent of novels published each year were by women, some 70 per cent of novels bought were bought by women, but that fewer than 10 per cent of novels shortlisted for major literary awards were by women. If great art was – or should be – above gender, the ways of promoting, choosing and marketing work of distinction were not.

Our simple aim was to establish an annual showcase of women's creativity and see what difference it made. We weren't driven by wanting to challenge the literary landscape as much as by a desire to celebrate international fiction written by women. The prize money came from a trust fund set up by an anonymous donor, accompanied by a beautiful bronze statuette, the 'Bessie'. After four years of research and negotiation, the first prize was awarded in 1996 with the mobile-phone company Orange as the sponsor.

Before it became known to the public, many – most – book people supported the prize. Others attacked it in the first year, gatecrashed the award ceremony in the second, and rang to check they were on the guest list for the third! Some still hate the idea, some have changed their minds. Regardless, the prize's world-wide reputation has grown. Hundreds of authors have been promoted to millions of female and male readers across the globe. Novels sit on bestseller lists, in bookshops and libraries, in ware-houses and e-readers, are on recommended reading lists at universities and schools, lie on bedside tables waiting. Multitudes of educational and literacy projects have blossomed alongside. And, in the last couple of years, other prizes have launched to celebrate women's literary achievements – including the Stella

Prize in Australia, the fledgling Rosalind Prize for Women in Canada, the Women's Book Prize in Iceland.

Are prizes the best way to support writing or reading? How do literary awards – dismissed by some as no better than beauty contests – contribute to debates about writing, imagination and creativity? Prizes often take up where word of mouth has run out. They help readers – us – to choose. We all know that there's no such thing as the 'best book of the year' – just the one that a particular group of judges, on a particular day, in a particular year, preferred. The best prizes focus attention on writing and reading. They encourage us to think about what we value, help us experience ideas beyond the confines of our own knowledge and motivation. Prizes salute achievement. Prizes sell books. They enable writers to live by their work and they keep in view literary novels that might otherwise struggle to be seen. Twenty years after that January meeting, the driving principle behind the Women's Prize for Fiction remains the same – though the context in which we have these discussions has changed.

Leading literary awards also have their eye on the long term. Publishing trends have always gone in cycles, a tricky balance of 'surfing the zeitgeist' at the top and 'jumping on the bandwagon' at the bottom. Chick-lit existed when we were setting up the prize – and the meteoric rise of mainstream erotica exists now. The elements of the writing that readers identify with, that make the books themselves desirable, are the characters' emotions – and these, for good or for ill, appear to strike a chord with readers.

But this isn't all there is. Against this cyclical, fashion-led backdrop, we need to celebrate different sorts of women's voices, stories, talent. We must push to the forefront novels that move and inspire and provoke debate, that interrogate big ideas, that dazzle with the quality of their writing. We must strive to ensure a plurality of voices is heard.

*

Twenty years ago we wanted to recognize 'excellence, originality and accessibility'. Nothing has changed. Except perhaps that we see even more clearly that these virtues can sometimes go hand-in-glove with popularity in the market.

The cultural landscape is very different from when we set up the prize and, given its demonstrable success in promoting excellence and women's writing, funding education and literacy projects, I find it odd that I am asked repeatedly if we still 'need' the prize? Well, yes. In the same way we need any literary award that celebrates excellence. How can the world be a better place if what is brilliant, inspiring, beautiful is not cherished? In other creative arts – where there is no equivalent of the WPF – the numbers of women represented have, in many cases, got worse rather than better. In American and British art galleries, only 5 per cent of work on permanent exhibition is by women. In theatre in the UK, the numbers of women commissioned to write, appearing on our stages and directing still stands at something between a quarter and a third, a figure no higher than it was twenty years ago. The number of women composers – and directors – is also something less than a quarter. Within the literary-prize world itself, still only twelve women out of 105 authors have won the Nobel Prize for Literature; and fifteen women (since 1969) have won the (Man) Booker Prize.

So, 'need', yes, though strange we should still have to justify it after all this time. And in 2013, where in countless communities throughout the world girls' and women's access to education – even to be allowed to write and to read, let alone publish – is under attack, the visible celebration of women's writing every year is more important than ever. To celebrate excellence, originality and accessibility in writing by women from everywhere; to encourage new generations of writers and readers; and to put outstanding fiction in the hands of women and men who'll appreciate it. What could be more important than that?

'If I had to characterize
one quality as the genius of feminist
thought, culture and action, it would
be the connectivity'

Robin Morgan

27
Susie Orbach
A Love Letter to Feminism

In 1972 I fetched up at the first ever Women's Studies pro-gramme. Located at City University of New York's short-lived experimental college in working-class Staten Island, it was an unlikely site for revolutionary ideas. But the faculty was young and adventurous. Students sat on committees, proposed courses, graded themselves and their professors.

Without knowing it, we were learning to take power. Because we students constituted the majority on departmental decision-making, we were transforming the institution. We weren't sitting on the barricades and demanding to be let in; we were inside, learning how to think clearly in a new field, with a canon to be made rather than overthrown.

Knowing what you don't want is one thing. Discovering what you do want is an entirely different adventure. Daring to think and enact new ways of learning and living thrilled us, but we had no model and we were more scared than we knew. Into the fear came conflict dressed in the garb of hierarchies of oppression and entitlement. The soft fuzziness of sisterhood fractured and we put our academic programme in jeopardy. We began to bond on the basis of enmity and factions. Our precious new-found world was in danger of imploding.

Like revolutionaries before and after, it was the fears inside us that we had to confront. We had to understand them and the ways they played out between us. We had to face the shattering of simplistic notions of solidarity, as well as the extreme disappointment and fury that we could now feel towards one another as differences emerged. It was perplexing, horrible and frightening.

We didn't, however, give up. Instead, we began to appreciate quite how much patriarchy was a structure undermining us, within and between women, as much as a political force outside us. We needed each other as we took on the challenge not to be defeated.

The most important ingredient in our quest to remake ourselves (and society) was each other. Exhilarating friendships took centre stage. They were a cradle underpinning our personal and collective struggles. We helped each other find and tell our stories as we were reshaping ourselves. Inside friendship we found ways to tackle our hesitancies, our fears, our insecurities, our shame and self-doubt. We saw how, unwittingly, we bound one another's feet and desires by imagining disapproval, fearing envy, not knowing how to deal with competitive feelings, difficult desires or uncertainties.

Inner conflict thwarted us. Internal psychological chains kept us in check and away from being as full as we could be. We feared deserting each other, the revolution, our mothers, our own inner images. But friends – my friends, my magnificent friends – were there, pulling for me and letting me pull for them.

Women's love, women's friendship became and are the weft and the warp of lives made together and separately. Always tender. Often fierce. Ever true. It was and is a lived feminism. Attached and yet separate. Connected while autonomous. A love rich and light. All the colours of the rainbow. A cradle for joys and sorrows as well as the everyday. A hand – several hands; a mind – several minds; a heart – several hearts to hold and be held by. Warmth. Toughness. Yielding. Listening.

Feminism saved my life and it gave me life. Feminism joined all our experiences together and made what might happen to any one of us comprehensible. It allowed us to transform difficult and potentially destructive experiences into new forms of understanding and solidarity. It enabled us to create different institutions and collaborative ways of working, and experiment with how and where we loved. There wasn't only individual failure or success *per se* but a sense of the inherent difficulties any one of us might encounter.

Without feminism, the struggle to make sense of individual lives – at work, domestically, with children, with lovers – would have become circular. Without feminism, life's challenges could and would have warped my individual experiences – as it did for so many of my mothers' generation – turning them sour and bitter, rather than into places of learning. Without feminism I couldn't have understood my personal dilemmas. Nor would I have had the capacity to reflect. Nor would I have ever taken myself and my work seriously. Nor would I have enjoyed my children so much. I would have lived, I fear, as so many women before me, doing what was required, of course, yet, in my head, having internalized a misogyny that would have distanced me from a *woman's* life. Phew. I didn't. I was lucky. I couldn't and can't bear to imagine missing out on the zany, wonderful world of women with our immense capacity for joy, empathy, chiding, brilliance and change.

'In Conversation'   Alison Bechdel

28
Laurie Penny
Saudade

There are more of us than you think, kicking off our high-heeled shoes to run and being told not so fast

The best minds of my generation consumed by craving, furious half-naked starving—

Who ripped tights and dripping make-up smoked alone in bed-sits bare mattresses waiting for transfiguration

Who ran half-dressed out of department stores yelling that we didn't want to be good and beautiful

Who glowing high and hopeful were the last to leave the gig our skin crackling with lust and sweat and pure music

Who wrote poetry on each other's arms and cared more about fucking than being fuckable

Who worked until our backs stiffened and our limbs sang with the memory of misbehaviour that was what it was to be a woman

Who dared to dance until dawn and were drugged and raped by men in clean T-shirts and woke up scared and sore to be told it was our fault

Who swallowed bosses' patronizing side-eyes stole away from violent broken boys in the middle of the night and vowed never again to try to fix the world one man at a time

Who slammed down the tray of drinks and tore off our aprons and aching smiles and went scowling out into the streets looking for change

Who stripped in dark rooms for strangers' anodyne dollars because we wanted education and were told we were traitors

Who sat faces upturned to the glow of the network searching searching for strangers who would call us pretty

Who bared our breasts to hidden cameras and fought and fought and fought to be human

Who waited in grim hallways with synth-pop crackling over the speaker system for the doctor to call us clutching fistfuls of pamphlets calling us sluts whores murderers

Who crossed continents alone with knapsacks full of books bare limbs clear-eyed vision running running from the homes that held our mothers down

Who filled notebooks with gibberish philosophy and scraps of stories and cameras to prove we were there keeping our novels and the names of our children close in our hearts

Who were told all our lives that we were too loud too risky too fat too ugly too scruffy too selfish too much and refused to take up less space refused to be still refused refused refused to be tame

Who would never be still. Who would never shut up. Who were punished for it and spat and snarled and shook the bars of our cages until they snapped and they called us wild and crazy and we laughed with mouths open legs open hearts open hands open and would never not ever be tame.

Sara, I'm with you in hospital, in the narrow rooms where you have put off your veil to count your ribs through your T-shirt, short hair and secrets and quiet defiance crying together that we don't know how to be perfect—

Lara, I'm with you in mandatory art therapy, where we draw pictures of weeping cocks and are told we are not making progress—

Lila, I'm with you in a north London bathroom, watching unreal maggots crawl in the cuts in your arms and listening to your girlfriend drunk and raging through the wall—

Andy, I'm with you in Bethnal Green, where you love ambitious angry women with heart brain pen fingers tongue and you have a line from Nietzsche tattooed over your cunt—

Adele, I'm with you in the student occupation, with your lipstick and cloche hat and teenage lisp drawling that there's not
enough fucking in this revolution and we must take action—

Kay, I'm with you on the night bus, half drunk and high drag-
ging bright-eyed boys home to our bed, where we watch them
worn out sleeping and whisper that we will never be married—

Katie, I'm with you in Zucotti Park, where a broken heart is less
important than a broken laptop is less important than a broken
future and we watch the cops beating kids bloody on the pavement for daring to ask for more—

Tara, I'm with you in Islington where you have thrown all your
pretty dresses out of the window and flushed your medication
so you can write and write—

Alex, I'm with you and a bottle of Scotch at two in the morning when you tell me that no man will make us live for ever and
we must seduce the city the country the world—

We are always hungry.

There are more of us than you think.

'She is a friend of mind. She gather
me, man. The pieces I am, she gather them
and give them back to me in all the right order.
It's good, you know, when you got a woman
who is a friend of your mind'

Toni Morrison

29
Lisa Power

On Being a Woman

When I was seven, I remember sitting up in bed one evening, sobbing to my mother because I wasn't a boy. Not because I was a boy inside, but because boys got to swashbuckle and command armies and be princes who actually did deeds, not princesses who sat and waited for something to happen to them.

When I was nine and precociously mad about Shakespeare, I wanted to be Richard III. Hamlet at a pinch. Not Cordelia or Desdemona and certainly not Juliet. I wanted a sword and a good soliloquy, but Portia was about the only women's part that got halfway there and even she was husband-hunting.

When I was ten, I remember my mum putting on perfume for the one evening of the year she went out with my father to the Croydon Conservative Ladies' Night. My dad got to go out with his mates every Friday night to The Club.

When I was eleven, I got a free place at a grant-maintained Girls' Public Day School Trust school and was able to take it; my mother and grandmother had both passed the entrance exam in previous generations while it was a private school but had been rejected because their parents were 'in trade'. The local authority, who was paying for my place, had no such qualms and suddenly I was in a girls-only place that valued academic learning. They gave me compulsory speech therapy to get rid of my common accent, though.

When I was sixteen, I realized that the girls who didn't make it to university almost all got shunted into being someone's secretary. When I was seventeen, the headmistress told my mother that I wasn't university material. At eighteen, I got a place at Lancaster to read politics and history. Thank you, Miss Cameron, for annoying me enough to make me make the effort.

When I was nineteen, I was ostracized by the University Rugby Club for not being a submissive enough girlfriend to the prop-forward, and for beating the captain of the First XV at pint-in-one. I knew they were in the wrong and stupid, but it still hurt.

When I was twenty-one, I came out as a lesbian and read every feminist text going. Whoopee! And when all the other feminists at college that year decided they were 'political lesbians', I seemed quite popular for practice. I felt vaguely guilty that they were doing it for higher reasons while I was most certainly doing it for lust.

When I was twenty-three, a friend complained he couldn't work out whether I was a radical feminist, a socialist feminist or a political feminist. 'Good,' I said.

When I was twenty-five, I was told I was the sort who gives lesbian women a bad name because I was too feminist.

When I was twenty-eight, I was told I was the sort who gives lesbian women a bad name because I wasn't feminist enough. Eh.

When I was twenty-nine, I asked my grandmother about her

life. 'I should have been a man,' she said bitterly. 'If I'd been a man, I would have got things done.' I remembered myself at seven and, just for a second, felt despair. And then determination.

When I was thirty-seven and running an LGBT organization, I was censured by the women's caucus for not attending their women-only meetings. I pointed out that they had consistently scheduled them against the political action planning meetings for the whole group, forcing me to choose between being a good feminist or a good activist, and removing women from the leadership table in order to complain about not being in enough leadership positions.

I'm grateful and aware that all these complaints are tiny ones in comparison to others. I've never been shot for wanting an education, or had acid thrown at me for not being a good girl, or been beaten senseless for being sexually unavailable. OK, I was queer-bashed once, but by a short-sighted bigot who mistook me for a gay man and was more surprised than I was. But even in one of the best environments for a woman that I know of globally and historically, I still spent too much of my life thinking I ought at least try to and live up to someone else's expectations of what a woman is, or should be.

Now I'm in my late fifties, people seem to have stopped telling me I'm the wrong sort of woman, or feminist, or lesbian. Possibly I've gained so much character momentum that they can tell it wouldn't end well for them. But this I know: there's no one way to be a good woman, or any kind of woman at all. We just have to keep trying and keep trying to be good to one another. I don't tend to listen so much to what people say about women and feminism any more; I watch what they do. I watch whether they help us to expand our horizons, or close them down. I want women to be whatever we want to be, as long as it's excellent in its own way.

'[Feminism is] a socialist, anti-family
political movement that encourages women to leave
their husbands, kill their children, practice witchcraft,
destroy capitalism and become lesbians'

Pat Robertson

US right-wing evangelist

30
Nina Power

So Much to be Done

My comprehensive school couldn't have put it any more clearly: the future was bright for young women, and there was nothing – nothing! – we couldn't do if we put our minds to it. It was a deeply positive message, one conveyed by women (and men) who'd experienced aspects of the bad old days through the filter of their own parents' generation – women being treated as second-class citizens, fixed gender stereotypes and the quiet, daily desolation of disappointment predicated on as-yet-unshaken assumptions about roles and behaviour.

Our teachers, and parents too, were baby-boomers – many of whom had embraced the freedoms that a post-war world had afforded: very few of them lived where they had grown up, including my own parents, who had left the outskirts of cities – Bristol, Cardiff – for a quieter life in the countryside, passing through an education system that was free and even supplemented by grants. Opportunity abounded and marriage – if indeed marriage was your thing – was for love. A kind of soft existentialism pervaded, upheld by the sense that there was something bigger at stake – democracy, civil society – and equality of all kinds, fought for, won, was central to this.

So life was good: education was the key and good jobs would surely abound *ad infinitum*. The next generation would have it as good, if not better, than the previous one. Other questions – about capitalism, about work itself – were put on the back burner. The demands of liberal feminism, of parity in an unequal world, were accepted wisdom, even where representation of women in politics, business and elsewhere was, and remains, extraordinarily bad. On the one hand, then, unimaginable gratitude for fights waged, gains made and the opportunity to be unencumbered by this very history. On the other, a feeling that the concessions made in the heat of battle might have conceded too much too soon, and may even have misrecognized the battleground altogether.

Coming across radical feminist critiques from the 1960s and seventies – on family structure, sexual oppression and capitalism, as well as proposed alternatives – was a revelation. Feeling dispossessed from gender stereotypes of an earlier age *and* from contemporary ones made perfect sense. The critique of everything was indeed a feminist critique and the revolution was not yet over! In fact it had barely begun. It wasn't enough to swap one set of norms (wife, domestic, mother) for another (worker, emancipated, mother if desired . . .). The system that underpinned and demanded different things of women at different times – to work in times of war, to stay at home when jobs were scarce, to rejoin the job market when 'it' needed you to, to work always if you were poor – was the real problem. Whichever propaganda was in place in any particular decade was always working on behalf of 'work' itself, of the system. The system really didn't care about your 'emancipation' unless it could sell it back to you for profit.

Today – as someone happily unmarried, childless and still indeed rather childish, yet 'professional' by certain other standards – I find myself returning to these ideas from the sixties and seventies. They may as yet have 'lost', but their relevance never ceases to diminish. Global capitalism never ceases to tear tradition apart, but it only ever gives back a faulty and incomplete version of the demands that radical politics, feminism included, makes on and in the world.

Until women everywhere no longer have to participate in this system that demands too much and returns too little, and are forced to make 'choices' that are really no choice at all, then feminism will be needed. The future that my generation was presented with at school and home is now our present, and there's so much more to be done. Let's just not call it work!

'Those who do not move, do not
notice their chains'

Rosa Luxemburg

31
Alissa Quart
Unnatural Mother

My husband was fifty. I was in my late thirties. We had lived adulthoods that did not include infants, except as metaphors. And then, like so many in today's America, we had a baby in later life.

It was a shock, but predictable. She had been expected, after all. At first, she seemed like a foot-and-three-quarters-inch-tall, inconsolable alcoholic. And then a small (and very pretty) pig rooting for truffles, with my body and breasts her soil. I wanted to feel the BabyCenterdotcom-like rapture – my small 'pine-apple-size foetus', as they'd put it, was now 'a bundle of joy', as they'd say. But it was hard to appreciate my new daughter, to see her through the screaming fits. To tell the absolute truth, I was a little frightened of her vague newborn gaze.

What made it stranger was the discourse of the natural and the essential that had accrued to motherhood in so many pockets of upper-middle-class America. Women asked one another whether they gave birth at home; whether they refused painkillers as they dilated; whether they held out against the dreaded C-section and how long they went (months or years) when breastfeeding. Our hospital paediatrician shrilled that all formula was evil. A distaff corporation of motherhood seemed to be looming at every party and every bookstore. Motherhood Inc.'s bibles clambered up the bestseller lists, its writers telling me what to do.

It was part of a maternalism that encouraged nursing on demand until children were toddlers, attachment parenting, and even following the birth plan of the former talk-show host Rikki Lake, who had co-created a famous home-birth film, *The Business of Being Born*. Lake epitomized the machisma of the natural mother when she said in an interview of the med-free home birth of her son: 'And I also had a goal ... to have this experience, to get through it, so it was really magical.' Lake and others argued that epidurals led to a cascade of unwanted medical interventions. There was a ravenous new interest in birth labour – sometimes a far greater interest than the workplace labour that feminists would once have privileged. They utilized ideas from evolutionary psychology to environmentalism to back it up.

I knew my mother's feminism would not ask this naturalness of me. It would encourage me to be who I was – someone who was desperately eager to rush to my keyboard and my bookshelf. But 'natural motherhood' was asking something else.

I'd listen to the bravura accounts of forgoing painkillers in disbelief, wondering if I should be ashamed of how much I had loved my epidural: much of the labour was so pain-free that my husband read *American Pastoral* to me during it. And I realized once and for all that I wasn't one of the mothers who could be called 'the Naturals'. I saw my gender – and myself – as something of a construct. I aspired to both 'do' and undo my sex.

That was part of why I was suspicious and uncomfortable with what I perceived to be a freefall into the purportedly real or organic. The counterbalance was the occasional sighting of the words of French *revoltée* Elisabeth Badinter in American popular media: Badinter railed against what she felt was the regressive, disempowered female identity of the total mother. I knew I was closer to her than to my cohort. For one thing, unnatural constructs – cities and pain management – have always seemed pretty good to me.

I was working against the drumbeat of naturalness, though. A little over a year after I gave birth, New York state and hospitals around the country had started banning formula or making it difficult to obtain. By 2012, twenty-nine hospitals in New York City kept formula under lock and key, in order to discourage bottle feeding. They didn't, however, offer the continued free lactation support to new mothers that would truly encourage them to nurse – the counselling that I relied upon. Indeed, I was utterly dependent on a lactation counsellor and a doula: for the first three weeks, ten times a day, I had to use leaves of cabbage to relieve an epic case of breast engorgement that gave my skin the texture of rotten oranges.

I did wonder where was the maternal bliss my friends sang of, mermaids of the health-food store raving about the beauty of these early days, from their culture-encrusted forts, lined with bassinets and Preggy Pops. I had been told no one was ever sorry after they actually had their child. But I *was* a bit sorry my husband and I had to cede our seven-year-long love affair to this vacuous little intruder, that we turned on each other like characters in a prisoner's dilemma, her cries the soundtrack of our anti-rom-com. I couldn't help feeling that despite the new title of 'mother' I had regressed rather than moved forward, as muddled and fey and out of control of my swollen body as a high-school sophomore. I looked back on the explosive birth of my daughter, emerging like a pellucid alien, as the most emotionally honest part of all this. That extremity made sense to me. Motherese's coo seemed false in comparison.

In self-defence against my own bewilderment, I became an embedded journalist in the Land of Baby. Even then, it took a few months. I decided I would 'do' and 'undo' motherhood. That would be my way of becoming a mother. My husband and I learned how to hold the baby to help with her stomach aches and ease her rashes. She cried less and smiled more. But I also thought a great deal about what being a mother meant, and tried to create my own version.

My own maternal variation came together when I found the first of many ways to reach my daughter. It was not through the promised and militated wonder of my rosy-hued aureole snapping into a perfect latch. Instead, it was via the black and white pictures I pasted on the wall above her changing table. When she saw them, and the tile coasters with similar black and white geometries, her body flexed, limbs waving. Nothing before had equalled her fascination at witnessing a black outline of a jumping jack on a white background, or a black and white chequerboard. Her happiness at encountering an image easily rivalled that of any enthusiast and certainly any critic.

In a moment, I understood her, or at least part of her. That was when our love story began in earnest. Our bond continues to intensify. It's now an absolute passion, though one conducted as much through culture as nature.

32
Diana Quick
Arms Across the Void

When I first became aware of the Women's Movement in 1960s Britain, we were the lucky recipients of education in a merito-cratic society. A grammar-school girl myself, I competed for a scholarship to university, and it was there that I first read some of the key texts, and started to think for the first time about what it actually meant to be female. Then, as I remember it, the feminist agenda was very much a political one, with an empha-sis on the need for equal pay for equal work, improved childcare and abortion reform. The Pill was the single most transforming thing of my young life, bringing liberation from the worry of unwanted pregnancy and allowing me to explore sexual partners in a way I would never have dared to do before.

The fundamental key to the success of *Fifty Shades of Grey* has to be its eroticism. Beyond the fantasy trappings of sensational wealth and power, it's a book that minutely describes the dis-covery of a young woman's erotic fulfilment. Its heroine is powerfully desired, and that is the great turn-on. She's lucky that her partner is wonderfully skilled in bringing her pleasure, too; but it all begins with her sense that she is wanted. She learns a new sense of self as reflected in his eyes. For me, as I explored sex in my twenties, the most startling thing I read was on women in love and their essentially narcissistic nature, in Simone de Beauvoir's *The Second Sex*.

> The woman in love feels endowed with an undeniable value . . . She is overjoyed to find in her lover a witness . . . Love is the developer that brings out in clear positive detail the dim negative, otherwise as useless as a blank exposure . . . 'I am Heathcliff,' says Catherine in *Wuthering Heights*; that is the cry of every woman in love; she is another incarnation of her loved one, his reflection . . . she lets her own world collapse . . . Small matter to have only second place if she has her place, *for ever*, in a most wonderfully ordered world . . . But this glorious felicity rarely lasts. No man really is God.

De Beauvoir asserted that love should not pretend to be a mode of salvation, but a human interrelation, and that the way to emancipate woman was not to define her merely in relation to men, but to 'let her have her independent existence'.

Some forty years after reading *The Second Sex* and attempting to live a more equal life, it occurs to me that I have been singularly blessed to make my living as an actress. De Beauvoir believed that actresses, dancers and singers had been advantaged over the previous three-hundred-odd years as the only ones 'to escape the yoke . . . possessing concrete independence in society and still hold[ing] a privileged place', because 'they earn their living themselves, finding the meaning of their existence in work'. She thought that as performers our professional successes contribute to our sexual worth: we are not therefore 'torn between contradictory aspirations'. The ultimate achievement of the greatest among us will be the higher aim of becoming 'an artist ... who gives meaning to her life by lending meaning to the world'.

I embraced that, and still justify my chosen *métier* by it in a world where sometimes I think I should offer more practical help. But when I think of professional success contributing to sexual worth, I come up against one particular crux of the gender question. Sexuality, its display and its practice, still confuses us. Sex, a private activity between consenting adults, is exploited and hinted at constantly in the marketplace, and not only for women, but for men too.

Yet we still do not have a comfortable vocabulary for the erotic: we market youth and at the same time are repelled by evidence of the all-too-frequent actual sexual exploitation of the very young.

We discuss and celebrate the daring of veteran actresses, then gleefully expose them if they are found out to have succumbed to the plastic surgeon's knife or failed to exercise away their middle-age spread. Most women's magazines still promote the idea of working hard to make ourselves look more attractive, and are largely funded by advertising the products to help us do that – cosmetics and clothes and pampering of one kind or another. Of course, I'm part of that world, and exercise and pamper along with the best of them, but we have gone way too far.

Music videos are a case in point, full of thrusting come-ons from both sexes. This is indicative of one wrong turn the so-called liberation of women has taken: the idea that acting like men, in its most aggressive, overtly in-yer-face way, is a sign of equality. Does anybody heed Andrea Dworkin's assertion in her book *Pornography: Men Possessing Women* that our sixties lefty permissiveness is really just another route to pornography? What is the middle ground between a joyful celebration of our sexual

energy and its disgusting exploitation? Why does it continue to
be so hard to find a balance?

I am upset that, in so much of the world, women must still
cover their bodies so that men outside the family circle will not
be aroused. I understand it is a way for women to move around
more safely, but will we *ever* achieve a world in which women
can be what they are just as men can be, and meet as equal
members of humanity? And this is without even beginning to
consider how thoroughly disadvantaged most women in the
world still are, doing about 60 per cent of the world's work for
10 per cent of the wages, and owning around a mere 1 per cent
of the world's property. Women in many places are still the
family foundation. Working with the childbirth charity White
Ribbon Alliance for Safe Motherhood has taught me that,
across much of the world beyond the privileged North, if a
mother dies in childbirth the family will probably collapse.
Education continues to be an urgent necessity everywhere,
probably the single most transforming force. A 2009 UN study
on the education of women in developing nations put it clearly:
if you want to change the world, invest in an adolescent girl.

There has been progress at home too, of course, but we must
not confuse liberation and progress with an abandonment of our
traditional strengths – discretion, collaboration, identification
with the other. It is getting on for a hundred years since Virginia
Woolf wrote *A Room of One's Own*. There she looked forward
'a century or so' to our developing a habit of freedom and the
courage to write exactly what we think; to facing the fact that
there really is no arm to cling to, that we go alone and that our
relation is to the world of reality.

So while we learn to stand independently, let us try to let the
other be what he is, and reach an arm lovingly across the void.
That has to be the way forward.

33
Josie Rourke
The Right to be Uncertain

I took over as artistic director of the Donmar Warehouse a year ago. As I am the first woman to run a major London theatre, there was a deal of press around my appointment, Within the year, it's happened elsewhere. I celebrated the appointment of other women – snowballing change, just as change should be. And honestly, there was a private moment of huge relief: I was no longer the only one.

Much against my expectations, I didn't enjoy being announced in the Donmar job. I found it personally quite difficult. I was thirty-four when appointed. Just out of a relationship, I had (have) no children and that, it appeared, was going to be a problem in the press.

This manifested itself one horrible evening when, discussing which interviews to do with our (female) PR it became apparent that she didn't want me to do a profile piece because I was single and childless. She was – I understand – protecting me from pernicious comment. Naively, it hadn't occurred to me. I could question her instinct to protect me but she was right to predict it. Within weeks, someone I didn't know wrote on Twitter that I'm a 'sterile careerist'.

Disorientation ensued. Something I'd never feared – talking about my job – now filled me with apprehension. The obvious thing to say is: men don't worry about it, why do you? But I did and do. Less about what I was, am, going to say in interviews and more in sensing that this characterization is now unavoidable.

Do you fight it? Expose it? Book a shotgun wedding? In my previous job running the Bush Theatre, I was young enough for marriage, fertility, family to not be on the agenda. Taking over the Donmar at thirty-four coincided exactly with the moment of maturity at which I started to consider whether or not I want children and, if I do, what am I going to do about it?

Do it or don't. Whatever I do will now be a public act as well as a personal one. Imagine: the first *pregnant* artistic director of a major London theatre – the firsts just keep coming! I am not coolly political enough to follow anything but my heart in such matters. Is anyone, really? But here's what shocks me: I'm not ready to decide and my right not to know the answer was revoked.

As a feminist, I've always felt that feminism is most crucial in private. In public, there are always people (men and women) to reason and defend the place of women. The discourse is clear, potent and largely active. We're moving forwards, change is occurring. I do feel that.

The private sphere is where I most need feminism's ideas. It's here that we ask ourselves deep and secret questions. Interrogate our hopes, ambitions and desires, find out who we're trying to please, hold up the current shape of ourselves against the images that formed us.

But what if we can't generate the answers? Not out of any political failure, but because we can't quite get our personal lives to line up. I found myself as a single, childless thirty-four-year-old in a culturally significant job. My personal life can't be – apparently – like that of men: partly shambolic, partly surprising and a bit provisional. Of course, it comes back to my fertility. And a (too understandable) fascination with how we do one of these consuming jobs and have a family.

Reading *Fifty Shades of Grey*, my first response was to feel myself in the company of a sort of Gothic novel. It seems so terribly important to the narrative that she was a virgin. I think that we're at a point in the story of women where something new will only stick if the woman has a very basic, portable history. I'm not suggesting for an instant that soft porn requires rounded character – but *Fifty Shades* certainly requires its heroine's sexual history to be an empty blank page.

Well, mine isn't. Nor is it easily reportable. But like so many parts of our world right now (and a lot of this has nothing to do with feminism), there is a problem if the 'story' isn't clear. Because I'm a woman in a significant job, I'm required to have an answer, otherwise I'm a PR problem. But what are we protecting me – or ourselves – from? Something hurtful, certainly – who wants to be called 'sterile'? And this charcterization will continue to follow me as long as I don't have children. Because I'm the first on to the field, I have to be so clear about what I present, otherwise an agenda will be implied.

We have this all-female *Julius Caesar* in rehearsal at the moment. It will have opened by the time this volume is published. I can't therefore tell you how the production will be received. But I can tell you what it feels like to have embarked upon it.

Phyllida Lloyd, the director, went into the rehearsal room not knowing what would be revealed. But she knew she wanted the experiment of an all-female Shakespeare. Already it has been reported as an act of militancy, of aggression, of revisionism. But I think that's where we are. We've moved on a lot but what we don't yet own is the right to be uncertain.

We can't walk into a room, let alone a rehearsal, without having or representing an agenda. Will I have children? I hope so; I have no idea. Will *Julius Caesar* acted by a company of women succeed? I hope so; I can't possibly predict. But it if it doesn't work, it will never be expressed as a noble and failed endeavour. It will be reported as a fruitless assault. I don't know how we will get ourselves to a place where we can be uncertain, where a blank page can be anything but a tempting virgin; but that's my hope. It's my hope for careers, for relationships, and for so much more.

34
Bee Rowlatt
There's Something About Mary

Mary Wollstonecraft was a woman so far ahead of her time, we're still lagging in her dust trail. Born in 1759 into a wretched family that didn't like girls, she became a world-class trouble-maker. She rocked not only the political but the literary world too. That was all ages ago though – here's why she still matters, and why she's still useful, right now.

Wollstonecraft is famous for writing *A Vindication of the Rights of Woman*, but her *Vindication of the Rights of Men* came first. Human rights are her life's work, before the term even exists. She hangs around with revolutionaries like Tom Paine and William Blake. Even better, she argues with them constantly. When the French diplomat Talleyrand pops round, she serves him wine in a cracked teacup.

Maybe it was the troubled background: her violent alky dad, her feeble mum. Maybe it was seeing her best friend die in childbirth. Maybe it was being forced, as a child, to sit in silence for hours on end. But when Mary Wollstonecraft begins to write about injustice, she goes off on one like a blender with the lid off.

Men are 'flocks of sheep' following the 'bloated monster' of a monarch; willingly enslaving themselves. This in turn makes women the slaves of slaves, who 'glory in their subjection'. There's particularly scorching sarcasm for upper-class women: the most 'vain and helpless' of the lot, with 'the strongest claim to pity'.

Reading Wollstonecraft is like sticking your head out of a speeding car window into a torrent of rebukes. She regularly gets so heated that she has to use an asterisk to blow off more steam at the bottom of the page: 'What nonsense!' etc.

Wollstonecraft's international thrills include persuading a ship's crew to change course off the Portuguese coast to rescue some stricken sailors; surviving the Reign of Terror in Paris (she arrives alone, in the same week that Wordsworth scuttles back to English safety); and tackling the wild shores of Scandinavia. In pursuit of a smuggled cargo of silver. With her baby. Has there ever been another treasure-hunting single mum philosopher on the high seas?

And yet, tediously, a recent documentary lingered all over her 'passionate love life', and her suicide attempts. 'Wollstonecraft let the side down,' it pronounced; she 'completely undermined her legacy'. In the style of a broadsheet trying to disapprove of tabloid prurience while running the same story with images.

If you're distracted by the notorious elements of Wollstonecraft's life, you're in some tasty company. Pull up a seat with all her eighteenth-century detractors. Nice to meet you! Here, on your left, they're doubting that women possess souls. To your right, they're asking whether black people are actually people at all. Some spicy hatred with your side order of fear? Cheers!

The rest of us meanwhile will be celebrating Wollstonecraft's philosophical clarity, her impudent vigour and her hopefulness. Why should we still love Wollstonecraft? For having a go; for living at a hundred miles an hour; for her 'ardent affection for the human race'. And, not least, for her uncanny knack of being relevant, time and time again.

So yes, she set out the founding text for feminism, and yes, she was all about human rights before they'd actually been invented. But she was also a tireless multi-tasking mother, constantly bouncing back and reinventing herself. And she aspired, above all else, to be *useful*.

So here's the test of that usefulness. Below she dispatches a topical selection of vexing themes and questions, the ones that just won't go away. Ask yourself: what would Wollstonecraft do?

Career versus babies?

Peasy. She just tucks the baby under one arm and off she sets, in a series of ramshackle boats, to Norway. In 1795. She knocks off a bestseller and reinvents travel writing along the way. 'To be a good mother – a woman must have sense and . . . independence of mind.' The woman had it nailed.

Your best friend says she's fat

'Yes, your bum looks big,' Wollstonecraft would have snarled, 'but who cares?' Her attacks on 'frivolous' girly types who live 'in perpetual childhood' are pretty terrifying. On a more chirpy note, women are hotter in their thirties (the 'perfect state' of 'majestic seriousness') than in their twenties. Allowing for inflation, we can now certainly bring this observation well into our forties. Nice one, Woolly! By the way, she herself was a dark-eyed beauty, in case you were thinking sour grapes.

A male colleague asks you to make tea, and you're not a tea lady

Announce, 'I have repeatedly asserted, and produced what appeared to me irrefragable arguments drawn from matters of fact to prove my assertion, that women cannot by force be confined to domestic concerns.' Or, 'Go right ahead, love – mine's milk no sugar.'

Your daughter thinks Kim Kardashian has an enviable career trajectory

Wollstonecraft sees sentimental novels (= reality TV, 1790s-style) as dangerous for a young female mind. In answer she proposes gentle humour, to show 'how foolishly ... they caricatured human nature'. Let's imagine Kim doing her tax returns, all by herself. Tellingly, though, she later worries of her own baby: 'I dread to unfold her mind, lest it render her unfit for the world, hapless woman!'

Can planet Earth support humanity?

Wollstonecraft doesn't have an answer to unsustainable population growth. But she is asking the question, years before Malthus gets famous for it.

Why does he earn more than you?

Her faith in human perfectibility may have been shaken by today's global economic gender gap of around 60 per cent. Even where men and women undertake 'different duties', Wollstonecraft writes, 'they are *human* duties' (her emphasis). Warranting a *human* salary (my emphasis). However, although independence is 'the grand blessing of life' Wollstonecraft disapproves of wealth and commerce. So it's unlikely that a pay rise tops her to-do list. Note: her words 'the interests of nations are bartered by speculating merchants' have quite the topical ring these days.

Boob job – yes or no?

'Please. Really? Don't waste both our time. And don't come back here until you've thought of a proper question.' She didn't actually write this. But she definitely would've.

You can't be bothered to vote

Wollstonecraft died long before the suffrage movement. But she calls women 'slaves … in a political and civil sense', urging them to 'share the advantages of education and government with man'. And of someone who flung herself headlong into everything (love; debates; the Thames) we can safely assume that she *never* would have missed the chance to register her voice.

Feminists – a bit shrill and man-hatey?

'I do not wish (women) to have power over men, but over themselves.'

We are campaigning right now for a statue of the great woman at www.maryonthegreen.org

'Taught from Infancy that beauty
is woman's sceptre, the mind shapes itself
to the body, and roaming round its gilt cage,
only seeks to adorn its prison'

Mary Wollstonecraft

35
Elif Shafak
Lazy Summer Afternoon

One lazy summer afternoon I was walking around Istanbul with a Chilean political scientist – a woman whose family had greatly suffered during the Pinochet regime. We had spent most of the day strolling through the narrow streets and alleys, talking, observing. Tired and thirsty, we decided to have coffee in one of the tea houses overlooking the Bosporus. As we sipped our Turkish coffees and watched a Russian oil tanker nudge its way dangerously close to the shore, she turned to me, smiling, and said, 'I now see why you write about women's issues. If I were to live here, I guess I would do the same.'

I asked her what she meant by that.

'Turkey is different, you know,' she said. 'It's not like in Europe or America. In this country, women need feminism, naturally.'

It was that last word, 'naturally', that baffled me, the certainty in her statement and the hidden distance. What was obvious to her was anything but to me. It got me wondering afterwards. Did feminism acquire a distinct meaning, if not a value, as we moved from one country or culture to another? To be more precise, were Turkish (or Muslim or Eastern or Third World, however one filled in the blank) women in need of feminism, while their sisters in France, Holland or the United Kingdom had happily moved beyond this dated social movement that no longer served any significant purpose in the modern world? Maybe feminism was a bit like tobacco. Developed and democratic nations, having consumed it long and hard enough, had grown tired of it. The rest of the world, in the meantime, continued to puff on this old bad habit.

Were we speaking two separate languages when we talked of feminism, women in the East and women in the West and, if so, how could the gap be bridged? How could we stop seeing each other as essentially different?

I was raised by a single mother, a divorcee, or *dul* – a word that had no positive connotations that I can think of in the culture where I grew up. My mother was a working mum, and an independent spirit to boot. She had dropped out of university to get married and followed my father to France, and then, with me in her life, she had returned to Turkey, hoping to go back to university and get a diploma. In the early 1970s in the middle-class, male-dominated Muslim neighbourhood where I found myself, all of this was rather unusual. My maternal grandmother took care of me while my mother studied for her exams and eventually managed to graduate with flying colours. Afterwards she became a diplomat; she and I travelled to other countries, other possibilities. But I have never forgotten the silent solidarity between my traditional, superstitious, spiritual Eastern grandmother and my modern, rational, secular Westernized mother. And if I have had the 'luxury' to embrace writing fiction as my great passion in life; to lead a seminomadic existence and live out of a suitcase for years, which I am still doing in a way; to refuse to use my father's surname and rename myself 'Shafak' early on; to get married alarmingly late and independently by Turkish standards; and, even after that, not to settle into domestic life but to keep commuting between London and Istanbul with my children and husband – if I have been able to do all of this, it is also thanks to the two women who raised me and taught me, even in a deeply patriarchal setting, to be a free individual.

In my understanding, the women's movement is first and foremost about memory. It is about remembering the women who lived, struggled, worked and loved before us, including those we have never heard about. The women's movement is a sense of continuity in time, knowing that you are part of a river, constantly flowing, changing, expanding.

I don't necessarily call myself 'feminist', although whenever I am in an environment where women are seen as secondary citizens, and/or the term 'feminism' is met with at best a smirk, I embrace the word dearly. At other times, when I am around feminists, for instance, I feel more at home – among family, so to speak – and able to criticize the practical, theoretical and philosophical flaws that have beset feminism. Mostly, I feel more comfortable with the term 'post-feminism', which gives me enough room to be an 'insider/ outsider', both close and on the periphery, loving and critical all at once.

At the end of the day words, like us human beings, are made of water. They can be shaped and reshaped endlessly. What is solid is our need for a women's movement, a conscious, multicultural, across-the-board sisterhood. When I say 'we', I don't refer to us Turkish or Muslim women solely; in fact, I don't even refer to women *per se*, but to all of us around the world who are knowingly or unknowingly affected by a male-dominated system. That includes women and men, homosexuals and bisexuals and heterosexuals; yes, all of us who don't quite fit into gender stereotypes and who have always known this deep down.

Patriarchy makes women unhappy, for sure. But it also makes men unhappy. Patriarchy can be more visible and tangible in some cultures, but let us not forget that it is universal. And so is the need for writing on women's issues.

'Storytelling reveals meaning without committing the error of defining it'

Hannah Arendt

36
Muneeza Shamsie
The Words of Women

I write this in London, where I have come to judge a literary prize. By coincidence, the jury will deliberate a few yards away from Queen's, the exclusive secretarial college in South Kensington that I joined exactly fifty years ago. In those days, this was the normal and desired career trajectory for girls at private schools in England such as mine. Marriage was the only expected aim and ambition, as it was for girls in Pakistan, my homeland. I had nurtured happy illusions of becoming a scientist. My parents told me halfway through my A levels that there were hardly any careers for university-educated women in Pakistan – and none for women scientists.

In Karachi where I live now, my book-lined study overlooks a small patio filled with potted plants – orchids, spider plants, monstera, begonia, amaryllis. This space is entirely mine. Here, for the best part of the day, I sit before my computer and a pile of papers. This room and my career as a writer are the fulfilment of a dream defined for me by *A Room of One's Own* by Virginia Woolf, which I chanced upon in Karachi during my late twenties. The impediments of gender that I faced were complicated by living between two cultures. My Oxford-educated father was an executive in a British multinational in Karachi. English was the dominant language in our home and our social milieu. My mother's first language was Urdu, though she spoke English well. I was educated there with Pakistani and British children at colonial-style schools, but in Pakistan little girls are expected to be pretty. I suffered greatly because I was plump and ungainly and wore thick spectacles. I was also shy.

Reading was my great refuge. I devoured American books such as *Little Women* and *What Katy Did*, which my father did not know. He urged me to read *Robinson Crusoe* and *Treasure Island* but I hated tales of shipwreck and piracy.

At nine I was sent away to boarding school in England, as my father and his brothers had been before me. This was the accepted norm for boys in our social circle, in emulation of the erstwhile colonials, but few Pakistanis sent their daughters. My mother was determined that her daughters should have this advantage too; she had been educated privately at home and thought it hugely inadequate.

I was sent to a small, caring school, Wispers. There, I flourished. I did well academically and also found the English were kinder to overweight, bespectacled little girls than Pakistanis were. The school was very Victorian but the headmistress urged her pupils to do 'something useful' with their lives. Alas, they belonged to a milieu where intellectual women were tarred as 'bluestockings', probably doomed to become that sub-human species, spinsters. The Suffragettes of an earlier age were considered a joke. I often heard sophisticated English mothers declare: 'Oh I wouldn't *dream* of going to a woman doctor.' In the sixth form during Civics I discovered that no one else in class, except me, believed in equal pay for women.

All this increased my self-doubt. I never considered writing as a career though I wrote with ease. I thought writing was something that everyone just did. My paternal grandmother, a women's-rights activist and politician in Lucknow, had discarded purdah, travelled to Europe in 1924 and written an Urdu travelogue. One of my aunts, Tazeen Faridi, a fiery welfare worker, wrote *The Changing Role of Women in Pakistan*. Another aunt was the celebrated novelist Attia Hosain, author of *Sunlight on a Broken Column*. But these books seemed very remote from my life in Sussex: I had begun to think of myself as English. I also became aware of subtle exclusions, particularly in my social life, outside school. During my year in London, I faced more blatant racism, though I loved the city and its cultural life: classical music, ballet, theatre.

I returned home to Pakistan in 1963, to a society I hardly knew and where an imitation of obsolete English mores muddled along with subcontinental traditions. To make sense of this, I began to explore that hybrid genre, south Asian English fiction. I knew I had more freedom than most unmarried Pakistani girls in the 1960s: I could work and participate in Karachi's social whirl, though I observed Cinderella-type hours. I married of my own choice, at twenty-four. My husband, Saleem, gave me a typewriter when he discovered I wanted to write. I was also encouraged by my two best friends, both London-trained artists who were armchair rebels like me: we followed with avid interest the feminist revolution in distant Britain. But I wrote in secret from everyone else, because I had no confidence. Years passed. My children started to go to school. One day, my little daughter Saman wrote, 'My mother is a writer.' Her teacher marked it wrong.

I decided I had to get into print. A celebrity relative generously gave me an interview, which appeared in the local press.

Soon *Dawn*, the largest English newspaper in Pakistan, asked me to freelance for its new magazine supplement. My editor discovered my interest in books and assigned me reviews and literary interviews: I became the chronicler of a new contemporary Pakistani English literature. I had no idea then that my younger daughter, Kamila Shamsie, would become a well-known novelist. Saman became a physics teacher and now she has written two books for children.

Nevertheless the last word belongs to my mother. In her last years, to try and cope with my father's terminal illness, she began her very first book, a memoir. She was eighty-four when it was published as an English translation and later in the original Urdu. In 2003, after she died, I found stacks of Urdu classics – often written by her kinsmen – tucked away on the lower bookshelves. To me, my mother's tenacity, her love for a literature and language that neither her husband nor her children could read, embody the suppressed voices of women. But my mother's tale is one of triumph. On the last night of her life, she rang my paternal aunt Tazeen and said, 'All these years I was turned into a housewife and made useless! I should have been a writer!' Such a self-revelation, at eighty-six, a few hours before dying! By her bedside table sat Kamila's novels and my anthologies – a far cry from secretarial college, where success depended on reproducing accurately someone else's words.

'The most notable fact our culture
imprints on women is the sense of our limits.
The most important thing one woman can do for
another is to illuminate and expand her
sense of actual possibilities'

Adrienne Rich

37
Hanan Al-Shaykh
A Pigeon Whispers

Saadiyyah was a perfect mimic and the only spinster in our neighbourhood.

She could even imitate pigeons and dogs. She lived alone in a small house with a garden, she made men and women feel uneasy, but she was loved by children, especially by me.

First, because she never closed her garden gate, allowing us to wander in and play, but on one condition. She warned us not to touch the white flower, which looked like a bell jar: 'It's poisonous! Deadly poisonous: if you touch it and then touch your mouth, you'll drop dead!'

I was the one who dared to ask: 'But if this is true, why don't you destroy it?'

'How can I kill something so beautiful?'

This sinister bush and her comments to mothers were what made Saadiyyah so different from anybody I knew or had read about.

'Don't compliment yourself and your children, calling them djinns and devils,' she once snapped at one of the mothers. 'Djinns for your information are solitary creatures. They hate badly behaved and noisy children. And the devils are majestic! One has to walk three years on a devil's eye to reach his eyelid.'

I remember very clearly how she once advised a young newly-wed woman: 'Why do you walk behind your husband and not next to him?' When the bride answered that men usually walk before women in order to protect them, Saadiyyah cried: 'On the contrary! How can he protect you, when he doesn't see what's happening behind him? Let us suppose you misused your freedom and blew a kiss to a passer-by?'

One day, appearing from behind a line of washing and perfectly imitating a chorus of pigeons, she said to me, 'Stop wasting everyone's time, girl! Excel at school first, get good grades, and then we will take you flying with us. It's a promise!'

When I was sixteen I wrote a short essay about boredom: it was published on the student page of a leading Lebanese newspaper. Saadiyyah was the first person to spot it. 'Girl, you write about *ennui*. How can one be bored while everything around us deserves to be reflected upon, even the cockroaches your father tries to annihilate! Never mind, you write beautifully, though it's strange that you do because whoever feels bored is usually stupid.'

For reasons I didn't quite understand at the time, I began to distance myself from Saadiyyah. She didn't seem to care. On the contrary, she said she felt closer to me when I published articles about how I was entitled to be liberated, how I deserved the freedom to make my own choices, exactly like men.

Wishful thinking on my part. One evening, I came home later than I'd promised to find my father had locked the front door in order to teach me not to come in after eight. I hammered on the door; he refused to open it. Saadiyyah asked me to come and stay the night at her place, but I thanked her and kept banging at my door.

At seventeen I fled not only my home, but Lebanon. I went to Cairo to study. When my father tried to convince me that there was no stigma in arriving in Cairo with my belongings in a cardboard box, Saadiyyah was the one who offered me an old battered suitcase. I hugged and kissed her and she said, 'Go, girl, go and show my suitcase to all of Cairo!'

I returned Saadiyyah's suitcase with some tobacco when I came back for the summer. But I found myself ignoring her desire to know more about Cairo, or about me in Cairo. I'd moved on. Saadiyyah to me was a part of my old suffocating neighbourhood, while my exciting life was happening else-where. The pigeons had finally taken me with them and dropped me in the mysterious, magnificent world of travel!

Saadiyyah kept her gate ajar for me. When I came back home from Europe, amid rumours that I had secretly married a well-known Egyptian novelist – already married, and twice my age – and was being kept prisoner in my father's house, she said, 'Listen, I'm here to help you if your virginity is under investigation, but is it true about the writer?' I told her that I was madly in love, but not married. She answered, 'Lucky you! Has he ever talked to you about his mother? She must have passed on to him her integrity and obviously her talent too.'

Years later when Saadiyyah held my baby son on one of my visits to my father's, I found myself asking her, 'Did you used to help girls who lost their virginity and were in need of it on their wedding night?' She whispered, 'Powdered glass! The girl bleeds like a virgin and the bridegroom, proud as a peacock, thinks, How lucky I am, my bride hasn't been kissed on the mouth except by her mother!'

I often wondered about exactly who Saadiyyah was. It took me a while to find out that hers was a tale of feminist heroism beyond all imagining. Now I think of her every time I hear the words 'feminist' and 'feminism'.

She escaped an abusive arranged marriage at fourteen and became a cleaner in an orphanage in order to put a roof over her head. By chance, she met a strange young girl there called Al-Khansa, who showed her poems that she had written secretly.* Women were not then allowed to write or recite verse, unless it was to praise rulers and political figures. Al-Khansa refused that. Around her all she could see was a tribal, sectarian society, corrupt laws and customs that oppressed women above all. This conversation with her new friend opened windows in Saadiyyah's mind. Her own little room became Al-Khansa's refuge. They wrote together in the dark of the night. They hid verses in the room, inside books that Al-Khansa loaned her. Saadiyyah learned to think against the current. She read about the women's debate in Egypt, about veiling and Islam, about political rights for women, about customs and traditions that were imposed on them in the name of religion. Al-Khansa would lecture Saadiyyah as if she were in front of hundreds of people: 'Just listen to me. If all of you understood the genuine practice of Islam, women could regain their rights and everyone would benefit – families, societies, even governments.'

But Al-Khansa was forced to marry her cousin. She wept as she hugged Saadiyyah goodbye: 'Here I go – the feminist – "with wings cut off, head bent down and eyes closed" just as a male writer, Qasim Amin,** wrote.' Saadiyyah stayed behind and waited for her friend's return. She never came back. So when her employer, a progressive woman, died and left her a good sum of money, Saadiyyah bought a house with a garden in our neighbourhood.

---

*Because she wrote poetry, she named herself after the great seventeenth-century poet famous for her elegies in the time of the prophet.
**Qasim Amin – a lawyer who published *The Liberation of Women* in 1899.

Saadiyyah, the perfect mimic, the only spinster in the village, now lives on in me. I read that a male poet complimented the original Al-Khansa to her face: 'Go, for you are the greatest poet among those with breasts.'

She answered him, 'Yes, and I am the greatest poet among those with testicles too.'

I hear Saadiyyah's giggles.

38

Elaine Showalter

Having it All

First, high-flying MP Louise Mensch resigned her seat to be with her husband and kids in New York. Then, in July 2012, Princeton University dean Anne-Marie Slaughter explained why she had given up a 'foreign-policy dream job' in Washington because her fourteen-year-old son back in New Jersey was having problems. Her article in the *Atlantic*, 'Why Women Still Can't Have It All', drew over a million online hits and precipitated a heated debate on the continuing obstacles to the woman combining professional ambition and maternal obligation and fulfilment in the twenty-first century.

These headline stories certainly brought up some of my own memories – trying to conceal or resolve painful conflicts over my divided professional and maternal roles. Nevertheless, the debate seemed like old news and somewhat beside the point. 'Having it all' was never among the personal goals of feminist thought, any more than it was promised by other social revolutions.

Feminism did promise women political and legal equality, the vote, access to education and the professions, then birth control and abortion But until the twentieth century, most feminists assumed that marriage and a role in public life were mutually exclusive. Neither the New Women of the 1890s nor the Modern Women of the 1920s believed that they had been promised a full life of marriage, motherhood and a career, let alone fame and fortune in all these undertakings.

Of course, feminists could dream. After the passage of the Nineteenth Amendment gave American women the vote, some women went public with their disillusioned realization that they could not manage to combine careers and motherhood unless they were very rich, lived in big cities and could get help with housework and childcare. According to sociologist Lorine Pruette in 'Why Women Fail', 'The woman who wishes to be famous should not marry; rather, she should attach herself to one or more women who will fetch and carry for her in the immemorial style of "wives"; women who will secure her from interruption, give her freedom from the irritating small details of living, assure her that she is great, and devote their lives to making her so.'

As late as 1982, when Helen Gurley Brown published her bestselling *Having It All*, she was promising the 'ultimate woman's guide to love, success, sex, and money'. Motherhood and child-raising, choices Brown herself rejected, occupied only three-and-a-half pages of her 374-page book.

No movement can guarantee that women will have it all. But the hard-won personal goals of feminism have been much more inspiring to me than the hype of winning the lifestyle lottery. Margaret Fuller wrote about her own troubled identity as a soul-struggle she would eventually overcome: 'The Woman in me kneels and weeps in tender rapture, the Man in me rushes forth but only to be baffled. Yet the time will come when, from the union of this tragic king and queen, shall be born a radiant sovereign self.' Charlotte Perkins Gilman dedicated herself to living 'as I would wish my daughter – as I would wish all women to live'. Susan Sontag declared that 'the first responsibility of a "liberated" woman is to live the fullest, freest, and most imaginative life she can. The second responsibility is her solidarity with other women ... She has no right to represent her situation as simpler, or less suspect, or less full of compromises, than it really is.' Even Lorine Pruette, who could not imagine that women could equal male success in a male-dominated world, believed that feminist daughters and granddaughters inherited the spirit of 'flaming audacity' that had inspired the pioneers' generations.

With that spirit, we don't have to envy the alpha woman who seems to have it all, or wish we could have what she's having. Like Meg Ryan, she's probably faking it anyway. I'll settle for honesty, solidarity and flaming audacity.

'Freedom is fragile and must be protected. To sacrifice it, even as a temporary measure, is to betray it'

Germaine Greer

39
Gillian Slovo
When it Started For Me

I was twenty-three years old, fresh from university and squatting in London when it started for me, and when it did, it was started by a boy. An unexpected turn of events: the middle of three daughters of a powerfully effective and somewhat ferocious mother, I was far more comfortable with, and interested in, women than men. Yet I was also shy, and so it was my then boyfriend who asked a local women's group if they were taking in new members.

An inauspicious start, to be sent by my boyfriend to have my consciousness raised. But as militant as they were (and some of them were very militant about men's interferences), the women in this long-term group said, albeit a little stiffly, that yes, new women could join, and when I finally plucked up the courage to ring them, they welcomed me with open arms.

I was with the group for years, never skipping a meeting. I look back and see my participation as a crucial step in my coming to adulthood. From my involvement with those women sprang so much: friends to live with; friendships that have survived the decades since; and, as well, a new way of understanding the world. Not that I was fresh to politics. I came from a family who lived and breathed it, and I had a mother who, unusually for her times, had taught her daughters that we could be as good, if not even better, then the men around us. I was a natural feminist, ready to enjoy candlelit reclaim-the-night demonstrations that ended, occasionally, in court. But the bulk of my activism had hitherto been defined by the struggle for change in South Africa, and as a student I focused on boycott-Barclays campaigns and an attachment to a Maoist group that had me reading theory so esoteric that it bore little relation to our real concerns.

What was different and also transformative about women's groups like mine was that they taught us to use our lives, and the way we thought, and the way we were, as a jumping-off point not only to understanding but also to action. Ours was a feminism that combined a passion for righting wrongs with an equally fervent desire for personal change. We felt the inequalities in our society but we also felt the things within us that stopped us from a full engagement with that society. Our monthly meetings (did we choose Fridays as a statement of the importance of our sisterly relationships?) were a rollercoaster of personal revelation and political discussion, intercut with hilarious sessions when we took to mirrors and plastic speculums to get to know our own vaginas.

I look back on us with great fondness. We were angry and argumentative, but we had reason to be and it mattered to us to change the things that we had always taken for granted. We questioned the subordination that came not just from the outside but also from inside ourselves. We took on that slogan 'The personal is political', going through agonies of self-examination when new mothers in the group accused us non-parents of a failure to understand what mothering was like, or radical feminists from the local women's collective patronized us as dementedly male-identified. We had the rage of youth and the rage of the way women were treated, and both were fed by laughter and friendship and a determination to change the world.

Did we?

Yes, I think, in many ways we did. We changed our expectations, and as our sense of entitlement grew so did our voices. If I look back at my mother – who as ground-breaking as she was never had the permission of other women to truly be herself – and then forward to my daughter – who expects to speak and be listened to – I see a sea-change in our women's expectations. And yes, as well, I see the losses we have suffered, the denting of a conviction that we could fundamentally transform the world not only for ourselves but also for all women. And then I look and see others coming behind us, different, because we helped establish the conditions that allowed them to be different, and I am grateful, once again, for the group that taught me not only how to find my voice but also to raise it in company with others.

Posy Simmonds

40
Ahdaf Soueif
one story

She targeted me. She was in charge of cleaning the offices on my corridor, but she took to coming in and asking if I wanted tea or coffee. Then she took to bringing the tea in unasked. Then she stood across the desk from me and talked and I learned about her one daughter and six sons, the last of whom was six months old when she left them all in the care of her mother and pawned her one remaining gold chain for the cash for the deposit to sign on with the agency that shipped her to this land of oil and dollars where she'd been for six years – and I'd been for two.

'And your husband?' I asked.

Sabdeen? Oh, Sabdeen was a wreck, a ruin, no good for anything any more. You should have seen him when she married him, tall and bi-i-g and always laughing and such a large suitcase he had, full of things to sell. And they had Ansar and Nisar and he sold and sold till there was nothing left to sell – and no money. So she took the flour and oil and sugar that she had in the house and made little cakes and went to sell them on the pavement. And she sold and sold and used the money to buy more flour and oil and sugar and Alamar and Nilam and Lakshmi and Nalan and little Selam came and then the very big winds and rains came and ripped the tin roof off the house and all the cakes she'd made and the flour etc. were spoiled and so she took her one remaining gold chain and went to the agency.

And here she was. The agency bussed the women in to the women's university at seven in the morning and bussed them out and locked them up in their dorm at two. They paid them $100 a month and charged them for their lodgings and deducted instalments for what they still owed of the agency fee. They took them to the market once a week to shop for their food for two hours. She saved $40 every month and sent the money home.

My son was four and I was pregnant and my mother – who had the big office at the top of the corridor – said I was ruining my life and had to go back to London at the end of term. 'But,' she said to my mother, 'Doktora has to work and who will look after her little ones?'

'Good point,' said my mother.

And while I was in hospital my mother paid her ransom from the agency and retrieved her passport and got her the UK entry visa and bought our tickets.

England. She liked that she paid tax and National Insurance and could go to the doctor for free and by right. Every month she sent a fixed sum of money to her husband, mother and children, every Ramadan another sum for 'rice for poor people', and every year when she went home she took seven saris as gifts.

With the rest of her earnings she ran a financial system that I never understood despite her best efforts to explain it to me. What I could comprehend was this: every year when we went to

Egypt for the summer she would buy two or three plain gold bangles. And every year when she went home she would pawn them and buy a bit of land. Then she started masterminding, from London, improvements and additions to her house in her village near Jaffna. I was slogging away at a nine-to-five and writing well into the night as cracks appeared in my kitchen ceiling and storms laid low the plants in my garden. She was doing the dishes and working out complex sums and plans. But I could hug my children every night and she had to kiss hers in photographs.

When my youngest was six she left me and went to work in a nursing home. Tuesday was her day off and she would come and see me and tell me while we gave my boys their supper how no one ever visited the old people and how one old lady cried all the time and one old man tried to run away in his socks and they found him on a hill and brought him back. Her great eyes would go liquid: 'But why, Doktora? Why? How can their seedlings leave their father and mother like this and never ask after them? Didn't they bring them up? Didn't they get them food?' And she would hug my youngest and stroke his head.

One day the nursing home called me. When I went she was shrunk in a corner, crying and terrified, and couldn't or wouldn't say what of. She let me pack her things and bring her home. And after a while she let me put her on a plane.

She sends me pictures. She's sitting on a chair in a bright room with a vase of coloured paper flowers on the floor by her feet. She's proudly showing off the ceramic tiles in her bathroom. She's in that paddy that she bought to make sure her family always had rice to eat. She's in a purple sari and carrying her daughter's new baby while a little boy leans against her. In every picture she has sons and daughters-in-law and grandchildren around her.

Her UK citizenship papers came after she left. They are in my desk drawer.

'But the effect of her being on those
around her was incalculably diffusive: for the growing
good of the world is partly dependent on unhistoric
acts; and that things are not so ill with you and me
as they might have been, is half owing to the number
who lived faithfully a hidden life, and
rest in unvisited tombs'

George Eliot

41
Martha Spurrier
Woman in Law

On the first day of my training as a barrister I stepped into a lift at Southwark Crown Court and pressed 2. I realized I had made a mistake and pressed 3. The man I was sharing the lift with said:

'What's the difference between a woman and a shopping trolley?'

Pause.

'A shopping trolley has a mind of its own.'

And so began a sense of sadness and fury that has, in one way or another, characterized my life as a young female lawyer. There are two things that are related. One is important and the other is more important. The first is women *in* the law. The second is women *and* the law.

It is sometimes hard being a young woman in the law. The reasons are obvious. There is a lack of female role models: in England and Wales women make up under 10 per cent of

Queen's Counsel and only 25 per cent of judges, the lowest percentage in the Council of Europe save for Armenia and Azerbaijan. There is a lot of boring and profoundly wearying sexism at the Bar. The shopping-trolley story is not atypical and rape jokes abound in criminal court robing rooms. There is no support for junior female lawyers working on domestic-violence and sexual-violence cases. I am sure that I don't speak for all junior female lawyers but I found working on those cases very difficult and upsetting.

One of the first things I did as a trainee barrister was go through the evidence for a rape trial. Part of it was the eight-minute-long 999 call of a heavily pregnant woman who had just been raped by her partner. That case went to trial, but many of the others that I worked on did not. I watched one woman run from being cross-examined and another throw up on the courtroom floor. They both dropped the rape charges. Quite apart from what this says about women and the law (which is more important and more complicated), as a woman in the law, dealing with those cases without any support, I felt sad and overwhelmed.

These problems with the profession are important and I do not want to belittle them, but the law fails women in more profound ways. My own sense of this failing came from the collision of becoming an adult with becoming a lawyer, an experience that crystallized my feminism into something harder, more fiercely felt and more compelling. I was a feminist when I was a teenager: I read Greer and de Beauvoir; I believed my female friends should inherit the earth (which has not changed); and I felt angry about some things. But then I grew up, and a friend got raped and another friend got hit and I joined a sexist profession and started representing women who bore the scars of abject inequality. If feminism hadn't felt real before, it became real very fast and it felt instinctive and necessary.

My first hope was that law was the answer, but I realized that a lot of the time law is the problem. The law hasn't found a way to protect women from domestic violence, rape or honour crimes. It hasn't eradicated sexual harassment at work. It sends women to prison because it confuses welfare needs with the risk of offending, and it keeps women in prison even though they suffer more acute levels of mental illness and self-harm than male prisoners. It doesn't regulate the sex industry properly and it hasn't stopped sex trafficking. It allows pregnant women to be held in immigration detention indefinitely.

But the strange thing about the law, and the reason why even on the sad and furious days it feels like the right place to be, is that it is one of the most powerful tools that a feminist can have. I think there are three reasons for this. First, the law, and more specifically human-rights law, is the most effective way that we have found of asserting minority rights in a majoritarian democracy. Second, the law imposes obligations on the state to protect women. This means that the police are under a positive duty to investigate a domestic-violence complaint effectively. The state has to put laws in place to prosecute people who traffic women and they have to make adjustments to the way they provide public services to take account of women's specific needs.

Finally, the law has teeth and its teeth can be turned on itself. If the state wrongs an individual, the law can enforce a penalty against the state; and if the law wrongs an individual, the courts can change the law. Although Parliament has the last word and judges in this country cannot strike down legislation, when a court says that a law is unlawful, the executive rarely dissents. One of the most striking examples of this was when, in 1991, the highest court in England and Wales ruled that rape within marriage was a crime in spite of the fact that the law at the time said it wasn't.

In navigating this terrain, you need to be guided by something. For me, feminism tends to be what I return to. Feminism is my way of thinking about and articulating a belief in substantive equality. It is my framework for being angry, for trying to change things and for sharing experiences. I find feminism to be a source of strength, empathy and principle, which is what I want from the law too, and that's probably why I'm so caught up with them both.

42

Juliet Stevenson

Emotional Waitressing:
'Ere's Yer Lamb Chop, Luv'

The breach between how we experience ourselves as women and how the world perceives us is known to us all. It was always present in my life, I think, unnameable at first, and then more recognizable in my teens. But when I became an actress and began to inhabit other women for the stage or screen, making conscious, instinctive choices in the creation of another female life, I found myself encountering this breach in more acute ways. Being an actress, as a friend once said, is like being a woman twice.

And never more so than now, in my fifties. As life gets ever more complex, interesting, contradictory and unknowable, the roles on offer grow more simplistic, predictable, two-dimensional and dull. Life is going in one direction, and the roles are going in another. It's a bit like standing on the up escalator and seeing the friend you were hoping to meet with descending on the down.

When I was fifteen I saw *King Lear* in a pared-down school version with five actors, no costumes and in broad daylight. Yet everything I felt I was and strived to be was spoken for me in that raging, ageing reprobate, whose rash quest for love releases such a hurricane of events that he barely has time to adjust to one reality before it descends into a worse. When the play was over, it was as Lear that I stumbled out of the hall. They were his words that filled my head, not Goneril's or Cordelia's.

A few months later, on my first trip to Stratford, I saw *Richard II*. It was another, even greater Damascene moment. In the thick of a troubled adolescence, this was a story that spoke to my incoherent internal longings and grievances.

Both plays chart the fall of kings, materially and politically, while at the same time mapping their journeys into a new consciousness. They move through adversity to enlightenment. The stories of these two journeys released the actor in me. That summer I shut myself in my bedroom and learned great tracts of these roles by heart. I was Richard. I was Lear on the heath. I was not in the least bit interested in either their daughters or their erstwhile wives.

It was nothing to do with wanting to play a bloke. It was the scale of their experience, the breadth of their thought and passions, that ignited my longing to personify them – to have their words coursing through me and out to whomever might be there to listen. I had found an expression that was commensurate with the scale of what I thought and felt in that burning time of emerging selfhood. The relative passivity of the young women in those plays, their imprisonment in reactive response, spoke little to me. It was the human, not the feminine, condition that I hankered to portray.

Five years later, stepping out as a professional actor, I got lucky. In those early years I was given roles that every actress longs for: Isabella, Rosalind, Ibsen's Nora and Hedda Gabler ...

These are young women encountering huge experiences for the first time. Each is as a cliff face, against which great waves of experience come crashing, and in the ensuing struggle to yield or resist each finds her shape changing – sometimes almost out of recognition. These are stories of identity in formation. As the twentieth century was born, nobody understood better than Ibsen how the social and sexual restraints on young women, and the imprisoning perception of them, led to the necessity to shake those perceptions to the core. Nora has to leave her role as mother and wife: she walks out into the unknown, slamming the front door behind her. Hedda, similarly compelled, blows her brains out.

For me then, as for many young actresses, this was a time when life and art were intertwined. Sometimes the distinction even blurred. My experience as a woman learning to make her way in the world, and discovering the shape and scope of her identity, was matched by the stories I was privileged to tell. The parts I played could absorb and reflect the complicated truths that I was learning. The moral weight of the playwright's theme resided in the character I was portraying.

These were not *my* stories alone, they were *everywoman's*. I felt useful, because I knew I was communicating truths that were common to us all.

Thirty years on, it's a very different story.

Since the age of approximately forty, I have had to lower my expectations. Roles for women become fewer, smaller, less engaged with the main thrust of a storyline. Often they seem barely to attract much attention, even from the writer who has placed them in the story but whose face seems to be turned towards the male protagonist(s), or towards the young and sexualized. Older women become mothers, wives, assistants, enablers or disablers of one form or another. No longer are waves of new experience allowed to crash upon our cliff faces.

Instead the tide laps gently at our feet, without much altering what it touches. We stand for something – we embody, if not a stereotype, then a constant.

The exploration of life, of what it means to be alive, is deemed to be pretty much over for the middle-aged female character. She has had all her formative experience: her shape is defined, she already knows all that she can be expected to know. She is confined to managing, servicing or supporting the experience of others. Husbands, sons, brothers, daughters are at the centre of the action. How many times have I, in the last ten years or so, placed a tray of food in front of the hero, and said, ''Ere's yer lamb chop, luv' – only to pop back into the kitchen? Probably only once or twice in fact, but often some version of this. The metaphor stands.

This is not the case for men. Male roles are endlessly there to match their maturing skill and life experience: the Master Builder, Macbeth, Othello, Willy Loman – all have great events thrust upon them, as powerful as anything that might happen to a young man.

But what about *The Queen* and *The Iron Lady*? Yes, two great roles for two spectacular actresses. But these are films about iconic figures who happen to be female. Much of their power resides in the marvel that icons are seen to cry real tears or lose their marbles. These are not stories that reflect the complex, infinitely variable experience of women in the middle of their lives.

What does all this mean for the culture we inhabit? Women, it seems, are still being trapped in role definitions that obscure and distort the scope of who we are. Our creative life expectancy is only as long as our sexual value. Women remain fetishized for the things that don't last – smooth skin, firm shape – while men are fetishized for the things that do – wealth, status, knowhow.

In an age obsessed with image and appearance, instant response and sound- and sight-bites, it is hard to see how to move on from such anachronistic perceptions. In life, women are breaking into new fields where they were once barred entry. Stage and screen lag behind.

It has been said that the struggle for women is to be perceived as human in a world that allows them merely to be female. Let's work for a future where the characters we portray, whatever their age, are allowed the full scope of their humanity.

43
Meera Syal

Eating His Heart in
the Marketplace

It was perfect timing, being approached to write this article just as I was coming to the end of a long theatre run, playing one of Shakespeare's iconic women, Beatrice, in the Royal Shakespeare Company's production of *Much Ado About Nothing*.

The play is regarded as one of his finest comedies. The central battle of wits between wisecracking spinster Beatrice and equally sharp-tongued confirmed bachelor Benedick is often regarded as the template for every will-they-won't-they rom-com since – despite the fact it was written in 1598.

Ay and there's the rub and the beautiful irony of it all. Exploring and performing the play revealed why, over four hundred years after it was written, it still speaks so eloquently to audiences today. At the heart of the play is a funny, unmarried woman who is admired yet pitied for being of a certain age and single. Sound familiar? Other women remark she is too 'odd

and from all fashions' to bag a bloke. Beatrice is rightly celebrated for her wit, yet warned continually that she will 'never
get a husband if you be so shrewd of thy tongue'. Prophetic? Or,
more likely, Shakespeare knew that some things would never
change or age.

Much Ado is often called a 'broken-backed comedy' because,
after the verbal jousting and flirtatious game-playing in the first
half, the second half gives us a shocking and brutal incident:
Hero, Beatrice's cousin, is due to marry Claudio, Benedick's
best buddy (both of them soldiers). He has heard rumours his
intended virgin bride-to-be has been unfaithful and publicly
shames her at the altar. Almost all the men in the scene turn on
the innocent woman like a pack of dogs. Her reputation is left
in tatters. Most shockingly, her own father sides with her accus-
ers and declares, 'Why was thou ever lovely in my eyes? Hence
from here. Let her die.'

In a society where a woman's chastity is seen as a badge of her
family's honour and reputation, such an accusation is tanta-
mount to social suicide.

We decided to set our version in modern India, in the city
that my parents left in 1960, Delhi, and where much of my
family still live. The play's setting in a joint family household
bustling with servants fitted India perfectly, as did the themes of
marriages arranged via families rather than individuals, the value
placed upon virginity, and the vulnerability of women without
protectors. Hero is motherless, Beatrice an orphan, and the
second act brings what is a near-honour killing of Hero. Given
the fact that a shocking 50 per cent of all cases reported to
Indian police stations are domestic-violence crimes, a *Much Ado*
set in India provided both a great thematic and dramatic fit.

Undoubtedly, refracting the play through this specific cultural
lens gave it an immediacy and emotional resonance for audiences,
and allowed me to mine all those buried memories from women

I grew up with: their frustrations, their muzzled desires, their curtailed choices. It felt like therapy, but in front of an audience. Behold the funny mouthy woman who scares all the eligible men away! However, there was always one scene whose power touched something beyond race, beyond labels, because it revealed something deep and recognizable to every woman watching.

Immediately after Hero's public brutalization, Beatrice and Benedick are left alone for the first time in the play. She is broken with grief. Naturally he decides this would be a good moment to declare he loves her. It's a beautiful and bold move by Shakespeare, to place a love scene in the middle of a catastrophe, and what ensues is a startling dissection of the unequal balance and misunderstandings between the sexes. Benedick says I love you, how can I prove it? Beatrice replies, kill Claudio. At this point most of the audience laughed or gasped but, playing it, I felt this was a perfectly reasonable request. You say you love me. My family has just been destroyed. I'm not able or allowed to take my revenge, so do it for me, so show me. Benedick says, Not On Your Nellie (but obviously more eloquently than that); and then says, by way of an apology, Can We Still Be Friends?

Are you with me so far, sisters?

Then follow some of the most eloquent and furious speeches ever written for a woman. Beatrice lets rip. All of her pain at her powerlessness as a woman in a patriarchal world, and as a woman in love let down by her lover, pours forth. On some nights, when she reached the line 'O God that I were a man! I would eat his heart in the market place!', I heard muffled cheers ringing around the auditorium. These turned into grim ironic laughter when she follows up with this killer line, 'O that I were a man for his sake. Or that I had any friend would be a man for my sake!'

Ouch. Yes, she's telling him to grow a pair. But more importantly, she's underlining the word 'friend'. Be my friend first, above everything else, including your own male ego.

When she ends with this heartbreaking statement, 'I cannot be a man with wishing, therefore I will die a woman with grieving,' I often felt I was in some weird psychic head-space: I felt that I was channelling a deeply felt universal truth that women heard four hundred years ago and it chimed in some blood-and-bone memory. The women in our audience heard and felt it too. And these words were written by a man. He must have mixed with some amazing women.

Of course, if one wanted to be post-feminist and picky, it would be easy to reduce Beatrice's argument to a bumper sticker. 'No, we don't want to be men! Aim higher than that!' And we like to think we inhabit a world where most women can fight their own battles, on their own terms and without men's permission. Thankfully these women exist. But so too do those who are still as curtailed and oppressed as fictional characters written four hundred years ago. Every night that I asked to eat Claudio's heart in the marketplace, I felt I was not dining alone. And when finally Benedick drops his allegiance to the world of military men and stands by his woman, in that moment a play about the battle between the sexes became a true love story: a story about the meeting of equals and the promises kept between friends.

44

Shirley J. Thompson

Are You a Singer?

Quite often when I am introduced as a musician to someone who doesn't know what I do in my professional life, they ask with great assurance, 'Are you a singer?' When I respond – a little tetchily because this is a frequent assumption – that I'm a composer, the response is often, 'Oh, I've not met a female composer before! Can you sing though?'

I answer a little impatiently sometimes, not because of the response from the person in front of me, but because society perpetuates images of female musicians stereotypically as salacious singers and angelic-looking violinists, and not composers and commanding conductors. Unfortunately, after over twenty years in the music industry, I've detected little change in this perception.

When I began my professional life as a composer in the late 1980s I had few female precedents. I was lucky to be commissioned to compose and perform the music for a major BBC

drama series. Scoring for film and television was what I had
dreamed of doing as a girl, never knowing how on earth I could
ever make this become a reality. I acquired this major commission after taking my undergraduate degree in music. Before
taking my degree, many people tried to deter me from pursuing a career. One belligerent distant male relative exclaimed,
'Music – what can you do with [a degree in] music!' These
kinds of comments were hardly encouraging and could have
demoralized me, but for some daft reason this eighteen-year-old
East End (of London) girl was not put off pursuing her dream.

I have to thank my parents for not proscribing what I should
do for a living. I had a liberty in this regard that many young
women do not have. At university it was confirmed that I had
a natural talent for original composition and orchestration;
however I still did not think I was good enough to take music
composition as a serious option until one of my lecturers suggested that I should study it by way of a postgraduate masters
degree. My confidence in the possibility of becoming a composer stemmed from here, but there are no predetermined
pathways to becoming a composer, as there is to becoming a
medical doctor, for instance. You need to know the 'right'
people, who can guide you into the 'right' circles and champion
you before you are taken seriously. Ironically, my naivety saved
me. If I had realized the elusiveness of the path to pursuing a
career in music composition, I may have been put off yet again.

Since my early commission scoring music for the BBC, I
have composed for a number of television programmes and
short films, as well as a substantial body of classical music for the
concert hall. Music for this genre includes opera, contemporary
ballet, orchestral and chamber music. I set up and conducted my
own chamber ensemble in 1994 and have had the honour of
conducting performances of my work with international
orchestras, including the Royal Philharmonic Orchestra, who

recorded my symphony *New Nation Rising: A Twenty-First-Century Symphony*. The symphony tells the story of London through music over a thousand-year history, beginning in 1066 to the present day, and the concept was latterly employed for the opening ceremony of the 2012 Olympics.

It was after the recording of my symphony that I was found to be the first woman in thirty years to have composed and conducted a symphony. I was also apparently one of the few women to have worked as a composer and musical director at the BBC Lime Street studios.

I am currently composing a series of works based on women in history who made a significant impact on their societies. I've recovered submerged narratives about women who have been largely overlooked, sometimes misrepresented and mostly hidden among the deluge of popular, largely male-dominated tales in western European and world historiography. My parliamentary commission to commemorate 250 years of the anniversary of the law to abolish the transatlantic trade in enslaved African people (1807) was the catalyst to this series of works, begun in 2007. The number of women that I was not aware of who had surmounted cultural, societal, economic and physical barriers to make pivotal differences to their environments surprised me.

The women I focus upon include Queen Nanny of the Maroons (who led a sustained and miraculous military resistance against the English militia for many years in eighteenth-century Jamaica); Dido Belle (who is considered to have been most influential in agitating for the law on the abolition of the slave trade through her familial connections with William Wilberforce); the women who refused to dance (naked, on the slave boat of Captain Kimber); and the women of Manchester who petitioned against the slave trade in 1800s Britain. These women were not fighting for the rights of women in particular, but were concerned with inhumane behaviour by perceived oppressors in general. Acts of courage, as demonstrated by these women, represent for me supreme feminist models that I find utterly inspirational.

Through my journey as a musician and composer I am learning to employ the magic of music to tell stories. For me, there are depths of emotion and the imagination that only music can reach. It is important to me that we, as women, tell our stories, verbally, musically or otherwise. Diversity in all its shades is the spice of all our lives and our perspectives can be fascinating. Besides, there are many more submerged narratives that we need to unearth.

45
Sandi Toksvig
FeMENism

In 1804 a woman called Alicia Meynell took part in a horse race in York against a man called Captain Flint. History will tell us exactly what she was wearing ('a dress designed to look like leopard-skin, with blue sleeves, a buff-coloured vest and a blue cap'). It was a four-mile race and Alicia led for the first three but lost the race. The reason? She was riding side-saddle.

Some while ago I was sitting backstage at a concert hall waiting to proclaim International Women's Day and legendary women like Ms Meynell. In the green room was a well-known celebrity. I think I had made some light-hearted political remark when she suddenly turned on me.

'Do you know what the trouble with feminism is?' she boomed, pointing a finger at me. It's the sort of question I like to think I am well prepared to answer. I rummaged quickly through the statistics in my head and considered where to begin – was it the fact that not enough people are aware of women of the world doing two-thirds of the work while owning just 1 per cent of the assets? Does feminism need to be clearer that it is women who provide 70 per cent of the world's agricultural labour? My mind wandered on to pay differentials, the use of rape as a weapon of war, the shocking figures on female literacy and so on, but the chanteuse wasn't waiting for a reply.

'The trouble with feminism,' she explained, 'is that it doesn't have men in it.' The singer leaned forward to press her point. 'If we spelled "feminism" as "femenism" the whole concept would do much better.' She headed to the stage and left me, for once in my life, entirely speechless.

I was thinking about her not long ago when I attended a degree ceremony at the University of Surrey. The academic folk there had kindly allowed me a doctorate without all the annoyance of having to study something first. Afterwards I stood on the steps of Guildford Cathedral, where the ceremony had taken place, and marvelled at the youthful beauty of the genuine graduates. A young woman dressed in her academic gown and mortarboard was being helped down the steps by her parents. In addition to being bedecked in educational success she was also wearing high heels; such high heels that she was unable to manage the stone stairs on her own. Her mother and father supported her on either side. On the day in which her mind was being celebrated, her shoes infantilized her.

I wondered what Elena Lucrezia Cornaro Piscopia would have made of it. Elena was born in 1646 to an ancient family of Venetian nobles. She lived at a time when it was not the norm for girls to study, but Elena was a precocious child and had an insatiable thirst for knowledge. Her father provided her with teachers and eventually arranged for her to be presented to the University of Padua for a degree in theology, despite the fact that she had not studied at the university. Naturally, a few priests objected to the very idea of a woman having theological knowledge, so in the end she was examined in philosophy and in 1678 she became the first woman in the world to receive a university degree. It would be another 197 years before a woman received a doctorate in the modern era.

Elena led the way that other women might stride across the global stage proud of their intellect and achievements. But lately there are many women who don't stride. I have a friend who is the CEO of a major corporation. She is one of the most able women I know, who commands her large empire with confidence. She is competence personified. An icon for all women who wish to succeed. Recently, however, she has fallen in love. Being in love is a commendable state but I find the change it has wrought in her disturbing. Presumably the fellow concerned fell in love with the capable woman, but she has begun to dress and act as if she were made of something breakable. Out have gone the rather jolly jeans and comfortable sweaters and in have come gossamer shirts and heels so high that her feet sometimes bleed with pain. She no longer strides, she simpers and leans upon the arm of her beau as if she cannot manage, which, in her current shoes, frankly she can't.

As I click across the world's pavements in my sensible footwear I find the disabling of women through fashion a mystery. I don't understand that a modern woman wishes to do anything other than step out with ease. I asked my friend about it. 'We might be feminists, Sandi, but we still want to look attractive,' she said. 'No one wants to look like a ball-breaker.'

I think how enraged the world would be if a young female graduate revealed that her parents had bound her feet as a child. If she had hobbled not by choice but because someone had tried to disable her into staying within the confines of her house. Why then are we not equally enraged by the shoes on offer in every high street to young girls? Take a seven-year-old child shopping and you will find a range of kitten-heeled pumps and even high-heeled trainers on offer, which help cement the notion of restricting female physicality.

The problem with feminism is not that men are left out but that women will never meet men on an equal footing while they worry about looking like a ball breaker; while they literally can't stand up for themselves. I'm not suggesting some kind of 'brogue-only' movement, but if we are strong let us not be afraid to look it; otherwise we might as well go back to riding side-saddle.

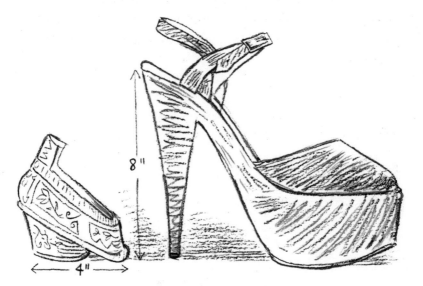

8"

4"

Posy Simmonds

46
Natasha Walter

Beyond Autobiography

There is an almost unspoken convention today that our feminism must be shaped by our personal experience of oppression. The most successful feminist books are often angry autobiographies. And what could be more directly involving than the story of a woman like yourself being moved to fury? Especially at a time when we are constantly told that feminism is outdated and irrelevant to the lives of liberated women, the direct testimony that states just how it is *right now, right here, to me*, is so vital in breathing fresh life into old analysis.

I've been moved myself by so much of this writing that starts from a woman's own experience – of sex, of childbirth, of work, of love. But most of the stories I've chosen to tell as a feminist writer are not my own. For instance, my most recent book, *Living Dolls: The Return of Sexism*, is not about my own experiences as a lap dancer or a glamour model or a pornography addict, because I've never had those experiences. When I decided that I wanted to map our hypersexual culture, I made the decision to walk out a little further than my own life. I wanted to consider not only how I feel about the pornography that seeps into every corner of our culture, but also the effect that this has on women much younger than myself. I wanted to consider not only how power still eludes successful, educated women in the professions, but why it is that many women believe they may be empowered by entering the sex industry.

That's because I believe that if we are to create a genuine challenge to inequality, we cannot just talk about ourselves. Autobiography breaks the shell of ignorance and hostility. But if we want to see changes, we also need solidarity, and action. I've been so impressed over the last couple of years to see how genuine activism and solidarity are growing in the UK. New organizations, from UK Feminista to Everyday Sexism, from No More Page Three to Object, are now mobilizing women to speak and act together, and it's wonderful to see them moving forward on campaigns that only just recently seemed to have stalled. With humour and energy, these organizations are encouraging women to speak more loudly and act more effectively.

But even given these new circles of solidarity, there are often women who are left out. There are too many women whose stories are not being told and whose experiences are still unheard. Is it possible for us to create a feminism now that enables us to work more effectively with women whose experiences are entirely different from our own? For instance, six years ago I met a woman called Alice (not her real name), whose experiences were about as far from mine as it is possible to imagine. She had grown up in the Democratic Republic of the Congo, where her father had been a politician. When a civil war toppled the government, rebel soldiers had come to her family's compound. They had burned her house and killed her parents, and taken her into a prison. There, she had been repeatedly raped by one of the prison governors.

When friends of her father helped her to come to the UK, Alice hoped she would find safety, but instead she was refused asylum. She ended up living without papers in London, which meant that she was unable to get a job or claim any state support, unable to get a room to live in or stay in a shelter. Desperate, and speaking little English, she started living hand-to-mouth, walking the streets of London from church to church, drop-in centre to drop-in centre, relying on the kindness of strangers. At one point she met a man who seemed to take pity on her, but after she fell pregnant she went on living on the streets, walking from one end of London to another until she could literally walk no further.

When I met Alice I could hardly believe that a woman who had survived such human rights abuses was living on the streets among us – and yet unseen. If we are serious about building a feminism that is working for all women, not just those who are like ourselves, we must ensure that women such as Alice are heard. It was in the belief that this is possible that I set up an organization called Women for Refugee Women.

Women for Refugee Women challenges the injustices experienced by women who seek asylum; those women, often the most marginalized and powerless in our society, who have crossed borders to flee violence, including forced prostitution, forced marriage and rape in conflict. I do not believe that women like me can speak for women like Alice. But I do believe that if we are to create a world in which all women are equal, we need to hear from women who are not ourselves, and build a movement that includes them.

47
Marilyn Waring
Five Feminist Vignettes

Josephine, who works with me, is twenty-seven. She says that for her generation it's not cool to be a feminist, though she is one. You can be 'political', but feminism is seen as negative or an insult.

'Young women feel daunted by how to change anything,' she says. 'It's so complex you don't know where to start'. She shows me the Bechdel Test for Women in Film.[1]

There are three questions:

1) Are there two or more women in the movie and do they have names?
2) Do they talk to each other?
3) Do they talk to each other about something other than a man?

I think that's a very effective message. All Josephine says about issues and 'what can we do?' is familiar. Patriarchy wants us to think it's all too hard. The first act of defiance has always been to disavow this.

I'm lucky: I have been a part of the Association for Women's Rights in Development[2] and Forum for many years. I see thousands of young women working on innovative projects – on resisting and challenging religious fundamentalisms; on becoming human rights defenders; on asking what 'feminist' evaluation looks like and influencing development actors and practices. Their energy, intelligence and courage keep me going. It's all been worth it, I think when I am with them.

In the past year I have written twelve large modules on Gender and Economics for the UN Development Programme for the Asia Pacific region. My definition of gender for these includes the following: 'In Asia and the Pacific, there is a rich diversity of cultural and social expressions of other gender identities, for example: *hijra* and *kothi* in India, *fa'afafine*, *akava'ine*, *fakaleiti*, and *mahu vahine* in the Pacific region, *kathoeys* in Thailand, *lakurn-on* in the Philippines, and *waria* in Indonesia.

'The term 'third gender' is currently used to describe individuals who are neither male nor female, those who are sexually transitioning or have done so, those who are both or neither, those who are transgender, and those who cross or swap genders. The "third gender" is officially recognized in India, Pakistan, and Nepal. The third gender is about *gender identity* – a person's deeply felt sense of being male or female or something other. A person's gender identity may or may not correspond with their sex (including their indeterminate sex).'

I think it's the first time outside of HIV and AIDS discussions that third-gender persons are visible in UN publications. I have upset some 'feminist' academics, who have made a career of studying 'gender' as a dichotomy.

*

The director tells me that the Dean of my Faculty, is not happy I am working on my parliamentary autobiography as my major research. From 1975 to 1984, I was one of two women, or the only woman, in the government caucus in the New Zealand parliament. I was elected at age twenty-three. Every document I received from that period has been retained in archives. Apparently my research is *frivolous*. Does he want me hidden from *his*/story?

In 2006 the New Economics Foundation (UK) declared Vanuatu to be the 'happiest country in the world'. In 2011 the World Health Organization-based report on 'Women's Lives and Family Relationships'[3] reported that 60 per cent of women had experienced physical and/or sexual violence in their lifetime by husbands/partners, and for 90 per cent of these women the violence was severe. More than one in four women experienced physical violence by non-partners over fifteen years. One in three women experienced child sexual abuse under the age of fifteen, and sexual violence over the age of fifteen. It reported two in five women were forced into first sex. The study showed the violence caused injuries for many women (including loss of consciousness for 50 per cent) and permanent disability for one in five of those injured.

Women coped by not telling anyone (two in five women), and/or temporarily leaving home (almost half). The study reported less than 1 per cent of women left home permanently because of violence.

So much for the happiness index!

Maggie has returned home from London and has become Jean's primary caregiver. Jean is her ninety-two-year-old mum, who is terminally ill. I was telling my cousin Janet this in a telephone call. Janet and her sister are now their mother's caregivers, and their mother cannot be left alone.

Janet says: 'We are living *Counting for Nothing*.[4] We have become the women you wrote about.'

Notes

1 www.youtube.com/watch?v=bLF6sAAMb4s
2 www.awid.org
3 www.ausaid.gov.au/Publications/Pages/3442_9413_2732_2996 _2379.aspx
4 Marilyn Waring: *Counting for Nothing: What Men Value and What Women are Worth* (University of Toronto Press, May 1999)

48

Timberlake Wertenbaker

Not Quite on the Verge of
a Nervous Breakdown

The email comes as I'm about to go to Greece to deliver a keynote speech: the subject is Theatre and Crisis. I want to say something about words, how they shift. The word 'crisis' itself moved from the notion of choice in classical Greek to disease in sixteenth-century English.

I'll try to show how theatre's power comes from the movement of words. When I translate I look for the word the playwright is going to shift around in the play, the repeated melody of the piano's left hand.

And suddenly into the inbox tumbles the word: feminism. Fifty shades of. My words are to be one of the shades. But it feels more like a word stacked with coats of paint. To be done in a week. I want to say no; I say yes. Not so much a shifting of words as of intention. Is my acquiescence feminine or feminist? Feminism as expanding time?

I call my agent. Do it, she says, just don't complain too much. Feminism as complaint. The lament of the Greek chorus.

I've never loved the word 'feminism'. Never been willing to call myself a feminist playwright: 'playwright' is bold enough. I'm nervous of isms, the claim to particularity. I'm no good at theory. I get my ideas from other people.

I call Harriet Walter in a panic. A great, passionate actress, a writer too, and her book of photographs of older women is an articulate statement. We'll meet after a performance of *The Three Sisters*; we agree it's our favourite play.

Feminism as a Chekhovian experience ... Moscovism ...

I fire off an email to my daughter's former drama teacher at Camden School for Girls. Are her students feminists?

I text my daughter: 'Darling, I've sent your money what do you think of feminism?'

She posts on Facebook: 'How random is my mum?'

Feminism as randomness.

Jo sends me an article about the Camden Girls' feminist protest in the shop across from the school. It's against the prominence of lads' magazines on display. The group 'is concerned that the racy front covers have two negative impacts: leading boys to see women only as sexual objects; and pushing girls into worrying about weight and appearance, possibly triggering eating disorders'.

I like that. Now a quote from one of the girls: 'Maybe decades ago people thought feminists were all old lesbians who hated men.' They do not want to be confused with 'the bra-burning militants of yore'.

I think the bra-burning militants of yore means me. I must say I have no recollection of burning my bra, but then I was flat-chested enough not to need one. But these young women are much more aware of the power of the image, the need to destroy the wrong ones.

Feminism as iconoclasm.

Harriet's about to play Brutus in an all-female *Julius Caesar*. 'It allows us to play character rather than worrying about gender,' she says. 'When a black actor played Hotspur some years ago, my father wrote a letter to *The Times*. This would hardly be noticed now. We hope it will be the same if more women play male roles. There's an irony in that we want to be visible but not noticed.'

Feminism as unnoticed visibility.

Harriet and I talk around the subject. The difficulty women have with handling competition among themselves. It's evolutionary, I think. Males are used to competing for dominance in the pack. They have an instinct for hierarchy. Women get confused by hierarchy, can't handle it.

But we can't keep acting like basic mammals, although we could take a page or rather a sequence from the penguins. I think I remember a film (but like many politicians I tend to rewrite what I see) in which the males and females kept passing this enormous egg, a future penguin, maybe just the future itself, back and forth to each other, keeping it warm.

Penguinism as the new feminism.

I'm in Greece; there's a general strike, demonstrations; chaos. Men and women equally on the streets, although on television, it's almost all men making interminable speeches.

Feminism as succinctness.

I ask the Greek women whether feminism is on their minds at this time. 'Women are organizing,' says Liana, who teaches poetry at Athens University, 'only we don't call it feminism, we call it democracy.'

In the so-called land of democracy (never mind the contra-dictions, bombings), Obama has just been re-elected. It was women who cast the bulk of the votes – 53 per cent. Women proved the deciding factor, breaking in Obama's favour by eleven percentage points.

Feminism as votism.

On a Greek island now, I listen to the tape of my conversation with Harriet. We talk about the lack of interesting parts for older women. I tell Harriet I approached a theatre to write a play for several older women and they said, 'We've already com-missioned a play about an ageing woman.' We laugh.

She quotes a former artistic director saying: 'I'm not going to put on a lot of Restoration comedies just to balance the gender casting.' We have another glass of wine.

Older women are mostly interesting when they're on the verge of a nervous breakdown, we agree. It's a rich theme but could there be another one? Not quite on the verge of a nerv-ous breakdown?

Feminism as the not-quite.

It's about history, says Harriet. If it's been done once and recorded, it can't be taken back. Her beautiful photographs of older women are there to record history.

Women tend not to write the histories, and certainly not the histories of the theatre. Feminists must become historians. Feminism as historicism. Invent a new word: *gynaelogos*, not to be confused with gynaecology. Maybe just: feminism as memory.

I'm walking around the Greek island with Leda and Demetra, two artists. The sound of the shifting sea ripples through our words. We discuss Greece. Education. The media. Feminism? Enough analysis, we say. Enough trying to get into a world we don't like anyway, media, power structures. Let's move into a parallel universe. We're women so we start with a fashion magazine: the clothes would look beautiful, the models human. Do it on the internet. And then do it for everything else. Question time by and for women. Woman's hours. Women need to seize the power of the internet.

Feminism as IT.

Feminism as a parallel universe, the PU.

What about men? one of us asks. A moment. Yes, yes of course; just keep them from leading. It's a bad habit.

Call it parallelism or simply universality. Feminism as universality. The word has shifted from the particular to the immense but this shift needs a poet, not me. I call on Emily Dickinson:

> *A WORD is dead*
> *When it is said,*
> *Some say.*
> *I say it just*
> *Begins to live*
> *That day.*

'The history of the world shows that peoples and societies do not have to pass through a fixed series of stages in the course of development'

Aung San Suu Kyi

49
Jeanette Winterson

Porn is Not Sex

'**Welcome to Women Looking For Sex!**

Check out hot, sexy babes who are ready, willing, wet and waiting to find the right guy for a one night stand or no strings
attached sex. You have it right guys, a complete database of
women all over the UK looking, indeed wanting, a one-night
stand or casual sex. Whatever your pleasure gentlemen, because
anything goes on Women Looking For Sex! You will find hot,
horny, sexy women of all ages, in all locations, looking for some
serious adult fun. And how is this for a kicker – you can sign up
for free! Are you ready yet? Sign up now and find that fantasy
one night stand you have been hard for. And remember, these
women are looking for sex! **Join now**'

*

'Buying or selling a second-hand old **women wanting sex**? Preloved is packed with nearly new and really old bargains in over five hundred categories.

www.preloved.co.uk › Heartsearch and Romance'

*

'Looking for free sex tonight in your area? So how does it work?

www.slapperdating.co.uk is the UK's premier site to find and meet up with dirty slappers in your area who are looking for free, no strings attached, dirty sex.

Simply register here and find dirty girls in your area. It couldn't be easier. The site is completely secure and discreet and can get you in contact with horny slappers who want to give you guaranteed sex tonight

ugly women, fat women, single women, all looking for one thing—

If it's free sex or casual no strings attached sex you're looking for – dive in, our slappers will go home with you tonight.'

*

'ISN'T IT TIME YOU STARTED HAVING MORE SEX WITH MORE WOMEN? It's so easy. Whether you're looking to meet and fuck: older women, grannies, mature women, 18/19 year old teenage girls. Black women, Chinese women, Indian/Asian women, married women, divorced women, women in stockings, women in uniform, women in kneesocks – WE'VE GOT THE SOLUTION TO WHAT YOU'RE LOOKING FOR.

Women who'll perform Watersports, women who'll let you screw them while they're wearing tights, rich mens wives, Widows who need sex soon … We've got it all for you – all over the UK – **YOU DEMAND THE BEST OF BRITISH SEX CONTACTS, YOU'VE GOT IT.**

The Best Sex Contacts in the UK. **RESULTS GUARAN-TEED OR 100% OF YOUR MONEY BACK.**

Categories

- Granny Sex Contacts
- Just Divorced Women
- Glamour Modelling
- Polish Sex Contacts
- Love Wearing Womens Panties?
- Anal Sex Contacts
- Want a woman who wants a 3sum with You/Your Wife/Girlfriend?
- British Sex With Uniforms
- Disabled? In a Wheelchair? Looking for Sex?
- BONDAGE / BDSM Sex Contacts
- FETISH CONTACTS
- Pissing and Watersports
- Enjoy Cross Dressing?
- Have Sex With A Mans Wife
- Your POSTCODE = SEX LOTTERY
- Sex Parties!
- Yes to Married Men
- Yes to Older Men
- Telephone Contacts & Best Quality Wank Material
- Older and Mature Women sex contacts
- Free Mature Videos
- Your Comments
- Sex contact Magazines
- Live old/mature women phone lines'

*

I haven't included any photos – Google 'women and sex' and see for yourself. The captions say it all: 'Busty Mature Slut Gagging Young Guy.' 'Hairy Bitch Shows Off, Ugly Women In Your Area.'

Have a look at the women who have posted up images of themselves in cheap underwear, squeezing their tits or flashing

their cunts and ask yourself what is happening here? Especially
if you are an educated middle-class forty-plus woman (cougar)
who thinks of herself as a feminist. Especially if you have daughters. Especially if you have sons. Spend an hour on this stuff and
consider your position – re pornography, re censorship, re sex
and sexuality. Take the porn challenge.

Fifty Shades of Grey did what? We know what it did; the old-
fashioned staples of Mills & Boon/Harlequin romance novels
were spiced up *Twilight* Saga-style. Romance with a bad guy, sex
with a werewolf, love with a vampire, an erotic contract with
a rich handsome sadist – and lo and behold, bad guy, werewolf,
vampire, sadist, all come good (sorry), and are transformed frog
into prince into loving kind husbands.

We know because we read *Beauty and the Beast* carefully
when we were kids, that women must just work at it and wait
for it, and their man will change. We know that women believe
they can 'save' men, and men still believe that this is true – so
if the man isn't saved, it's the fault of the cold bitch he married
or the bitch on the make he's fucking.

We didn't read *Bluebeard* as carefully as we should have done.

But Angela Carter did. *The Sadeian Woman* – her late-seventies
response to pornography is not a single reading of either the
pornographic impulse or its effects on men and women. She is
interested in sadism – and its necessary foil, masochism (gagging
for it, girls). She wonders if this is really about gender, and what
we feel about de Sade's women, who are as brutal and merciless
as his men. The only crime in Sade-porn is a good deed.

The Bluebeard story is a compact version of the thousands of
pages of de Sade pornography. Mutilation, degradation, humiliation, murder, save the perpetrator from the pain of loving.
Sometimes they save the victim too. If I am punished for my
desires I can extinguish the pain of feeling them. If hurt and
pleasure become the same thing I don't have to face what hurt

and pleasure mean to me in their own right. Fusing opposing feelings avoids ever feeling the feelings I am too terrified to feel.

Angela Carter was writing before there was such a thing as internet porn. Porn is no longer top-shelf or sleazy cinema or long boring reads through an eighteenth-century psychopath jerking off in jail. Nobody wants de Sade's musings on politics and liberty – they just want the bitch spiked.

Porn is as fast and guilt-free as firing up your laptop. The most effort you need to make is unzipping your jeans or lifting your skirt.

The two-minute orgasm.

Women are the new consumers of porn. Especially women under forty. Especially women under twenty-five. Capitalism is great at spotting the next market. And all in the name of free-dom and liberation. If a woman pays to see herself as a sex object then the market is operating and she can't be a victim.

It's all about choice, girls, right?

But. I'm not going to line up all the arguments about porn as an industry – porn as money and power, strutting around as pleasure. Or porn as a reinforcer of oppressive male values. Or porn as a destructive force on the developing self-image of teenagers, boys or girls. Or porn as a failure of imagination.

Porn is addictive – that is more frightening and interesting to me than anything else we can say about porn. Porn will wreck lives like any other addiction. Porn is not sex. Porn is a highly toxic, addictive substance that uses the excitement/satisfaction pathways in the brain to addict the user.

Porn is image-based humiliation and violence that calls itself adult play.

You cannot start or maintain a bonded loving sexual rela-tionship with another human being if you are addicted to porn.

What porn ruins is a healthy sexual response – desire and sat-isfaction. And what porn destroys is love.

Is that what we want for our men, our kids, ourselves?

Angela Carter: 'The holy terror of love that we find in both men and women.'

Emma Goldman: 'The most vital right is the right to love and be loved.'

50
Xīnrán

A good Chinese woman in five simple but powerful Chinese characters

After over fifty years of being weathered by Chinese culture, of learning and struggling with the disparities between five thousand-plus years of Chinese tradition and newly globalized popularity, I have just realized that the principle of being a good Chinese woman has been deeply rooted in five simple but powerful Chinese characters. It seems we have followed them one by one, generation by generation, from 1500 BCE until yesterday – some Chinese might urge me to say, 'Until today!'

Here are the five characters:

好 (Hao) good = 女 woman + 子child/son

As a little girl, my everyday life was clearly divided between good and bad by parents and teachers. My grandmother said to me, 'You have to be good as the character shows: a female child is about being good!' I can't remember anything I did that was in 'my own interests': I could only have these in my dreams. Sometimes I wondered, How about 'male plus child'? But that wasn't in the Chinese dictionary. Maybe this is why a Chinese boy has the right to follow his own wishes and be naughty.

I really believed in this interpretation of the 'good', until I became a journalist in the 1980s. Some country women I interviewed told me they had to have a son for their husband's family tree: otherwise they wouldn't be 'good' women! Their elders had warned them: 'Look at the character 好 (Hao) good: it is made up of a woman and a son together. Without sons, women cannot be good!'

妙 (Miao) wonderful = 少 youth + 女 female

Compared to English-speaking Western culture, conventional Chinese culture has very different views on what it means to be a wonderful woman. The golden age of a Chinese woman is between twelve and thirty: until the 1980s being a virgin was the most significant aspect of this age. Many Chinese girls treat virginity as an invaluable power for getting what they want for their future: from jobs and material possessions to rich men! As the old Chinese saying goes: a woman past youth is like a *fresh green* turned *dry yellow*.

That 'wonderful' was never part of my young life: my golden age was burned black by the Cultural Revolution. I am still looking for my *fresh green* in my *dry yellow* age. I hope my writing, charity work and worldwide travel can recover my lost 'wonderful'.

嫁 (Jia) marriage = 女 female + 家 home

Words in China are meaningful and expected to define existence. The character 'marriage' for men is 娶 (Qu) which is equivalent to 'take woman home'. But 'marriage' in the feminine version, 嫁 (Jia), stands for the family: therefore Chinese women used to be ordered after marriage not to leave the precincts of the home!

Since Mao Zedong in 1949 gave 'half the Chinese sky' to women, many urban women have now taken *men* home in marriage. But in the poor rural areas, women villagers are still living confined to their home ground and are trapped in the meaning of marriage!

妇 (Fu) woman/housewife = 女 female + 扫帚 broom

Everyone can see what women's duty is from this character: after marriage, 24/7 housework and toil! This is, of course, not only a Chinese condition. In every society and culture, despite a century of women's liberation movements, women are responsible for managing the home. Is it fair for a woman to bring up children and manage the man's family for him? If it isn't, then she would have to state clearly, 'Sorry, I don't do housework.'

If I had power, I would like to use it for two things: to set up a course for teenagers, both girls and boys, where they would learn what running a family really means in daily life – from cleaning, to cooking and caring. I would like to create a system that converts housework into a professional, paid career!

安 (An) peace = 宀 roof + 女 female

To be honest, I am still not sure I yet understand this word correctly. There are many conflicting interpretations. But the bottom line is that peace, here, is defined from a male point of view. A man can have a peaceful life, if he has woman at home for his needs. A man can live in peace if his woman stays under his roof. A man will obtain peace if he can assure his woman's well-being beneath his roof . . .

If a woman can bring peace to a man's life, as the Chinese believe, what can a man give to a woman to bring peace into her life? Apart from money and sex, what else do women need from men? I wonder how many men know the answer to that, before they take a woman home to create a mutual future!

Health, peace and joy are what we need in love and in order to create a family. Every Chinese woman can hardly expect that in a country that numbers over 1.3 billion people, many of whom have been forced to speed-travel over five-hundred years in a mere thirty. Uneven development has made that journey even more dizzying in the countryside than in the cities.

Pussy Riot

'Become a Feminist!'

'Virgin Mary, Mother of God
Become a feminist
Become a feminist, become a feminist!'
From 'Virgin Mary, Put Putin Away' (punk prayer)

*Extract from the trial of Pussy Riot: from the closing courtroom state-
ment of Nadezhda Tolokonnikova (Nadja):*

By and large, the three members of Pussy Riot are not the ones
on trial here. If we were, this event would hardly be so significant. This is a trial of the entire political system of the Russian
Federation, which, to its great misfortune, enjoys showing the
state's cruelty towards the individual, and its indifference towards
human honour and dignity, repeating all of the worst moments
of Russian history. To my deep regret, this poor excuse for a
judicial process approaches Stalin's troikas. We, too, have only

an interrogator, a judge and a prosecutor. Furthermore, this repressive act is based on political orders from above that completely dictate the words, deeds and decisions of these three judicial figures.

What was behind our performance at the Cathedral of Christ the Saviour and the subsequent trial? Nothing other than the autocratic political system. Pussy Riot's performances can either be called dissident art, or political action that engages art forms. Either way, our performances are a kind of civic activity amid the repressions of a corporate political system that directs its power against basic human rights, and civil and political liberties. The young people who have been flayed by the systematic eradication of freedoms perpetrated during the aughts have now risen against the state. We were searching for real sincerity and simplicity, and we found these qualities in the *yurodstvo* [holy foolishness] of punk.

Passion, total honesty and naivety are superior to the hypocrisy, mendacity and false modesty that are used to disguise crime. The so-called leading figures of our state stand in the cathedral with righteous faces on, but, through their cunning, their sin is greater than our own. We put on political punk performances in response to a government that is rife with rigidity, reticence and caste-like hierarchical structures. It is so clearly invested in serving only narrow corporate interests, it makes us sick just to breathe Russian air. We categorically oppose the following, and this forces us to act and live politically: the use of coercive and forceful methods for regulating social processes, a situation in which the most important political institutions are the disciplinary structures of the state; the security agencies (the army, police and secret services) and their corresponding means of ensuring political 'stability' (prisons, pre-emptive detention, all the mechanisms of strict control over the citizenry); forcibly imposed civic passivity among the majority of the population;

the complete dominance of the executive branch over the legislative and judicial branches.

Moreover, we are deeply frustrated by the scandalous dearth of political culture, which comes as the result of fear and is kept down through the conscious efforts of the government and its servants (such as Patriarch Kirill: 'Orthodox Christians do not attend rallies') and by the scandalous weakness of horizontal ties within our society. We do not like the fact that the state so easily manipulates public opinion by means of its strict control over the majority of media outlets (a particularly vivid example of this manipulation is the unprecedentedly insolent and distorted campaign against Pussy Riot appearing in practically every Russian media outlet).

Despite the fact that we find ourselves in an essentially authoritarian situation, living under authoritarian rule, I see this system crumbling in the face of three members of Pussy Riot. What the system anticipated did not occur. Russia does not condemn us, and with each passing day, more and more people believe in us and believe that we should be free, and not behind bars. I see this in the people I meet. I meet people who work for the system, who work in its institutions; I see people who are incarcerated. Every day I meet our supporters who wish us luck and, above all, freedom. They say what we did was justified. More and more people tell us that although they earlier had doubts about whether we had the right to do what we did, with each passing day, more and more people tell us that time has shown that our political gesture was correct – that we opened the wounds of this political system, and struck directly at the hornets' nest ...

These people try to relieve our suffering as much they can, and we are very grateful to them. We are also grateful to everyone who speaks out in support of us on the outside. There are many supporters, and I know it. I know that a great number of Orthodox Christians speak out on our behalf, the ones who gather near the court in particular. They pray for us; they pray for the imprisoned members of Pussy Riot. We've seen the little booklets the Orthodox hand out that contain prayers for the imprisoned. This fact alone demonstrates that there is no single, unified group of Orthodox believers, as the prosecutor would like to insist. Such a unified group does not exist. Today, more and more believers have come to the defence of Pussy Riot. They don't think that what we did warrants a five-month term in a pre-trial detention centre, let alone the three years in prison the prosecutor has called for. Every day, more people come to understand that if the system is attacking with such vehemence the three young women who performed in the Cathedral of Christ the Saviour for forty seconds, it only means that this system fears the truth, sincerity and straightforwardness we represent. We have never used cunning during these proceedings. Meanwhile, our opponents are too often cunning, and people sense this. Indeed, the truth has an ontological, existential superiority over deception, and this is even described in the Bible, particularly in the Old Testament. The paths of truth always triumph over the paths of cunning, guile and deception. Every day, truth grows more victorious, despite the fact that we remain behind bars and will probably be here for a long time.

Yesterday, Madonna performed in Moscow with 'Pussy Riot' written on her back. More and more people see that we are held here illegally and on false pretences. This amazes me. I am amazed that truth really does triumph over deception. Despite the fact that we are physically here, we are freer than everyone sitting across from us on the side of the prosecution. We can say anything we want and we do say everything we want. The prosecution can only say what they are permitted to say by political censorship. They can't say the punk prayer, 'Virgin Mary, Put Putin Away', they can't utter a single line of our punk prayer that deals with the political system.

Alice Stride

Saving the Bush

This piece was chosen as the winning entry in Virago's competition asking people aged twenty-five and under what feminism means to them.

*

My little sister was born when I was eight. I was thrilled. A girl! Like me! With a vagina! We would dismantle the patriarchy at home! We would smash the invisible system that meant I had to be tidy and helpful because that was what was expected of me, while my three brothers ran riot and broke my stuff (I was already painfully aware of the shitty unfairness of expected gender roles).

I was the first to hold her, beating the others out of the way (the patriarchy was being dismantled already!). She had a big, squashed red moon face, like a sun-burned grub in swaddling. She was hideous; I fell in love. Seventeen years on, and she has grown into an intelligent, self-assured, beautiful young woman. I would die for her.

However, the problem with being a big sister – particularly

one almost a decade older – is that I have been there, done that, done him, got the T-shirt, the STI-test and fucked up a billion times over. I don't want her to do the same. I want to guard her from what she thinks she wants: fire-fierce, protective feelings. She resents that, and I would too.

But, the thing is, the world she is in now is more frightening than the one that I inhabited as a teenager. It is more shiny, more glamorous, more false and aggressive, and in some ways more unfair to its young women than we can fathom. It is too much, too young.

A few months ago, I was on the loo while she was in the shower (yes, we are that kind of family). When she stepped out, I saw that she had no pubic hair. None. Not a wisp. Bald.

'What have you done?' I cried.

'What do you mean?'

'WHERE ARE YOUR PUBES?'

'This is what everyone does. All my friends do this.'

'Why?'

She wrapped a towel around herself and shrugged. 'I don't know. We all do it.'

'For the boys?'

'I don't know. It's just what everyone does.' She walked out. I stayed sitting on the loo, shocked. I almost forgot to wipe my bum.

Of course, I understand that for most teenage girls, fitting in with your peers is your life's sole purpose. I was the same, though for me fitting in was wearing a homemade T-shirt at a gig – not making myself look like a porn star. My sister and her friends are identikit Topshop babes. They all look lovely, but they look . . . the same.

'Being a teenager is the best time to look ridiculous. When you're a grown-up you can't always wear a homemade tutu over your trousers. Unless you're a ballerina,' I told her, imploringly. She stared at me, witheringly. You're too old to understand, her look said.

But this is serious shit. The individuality of teenage girls today is being weeded out by a celebrity-obsessed culture that is more acute than it was ten years ago, the pressures increasingly intense. When I was sixteen, trashy magazines weren't as prevalent, pop-stars and actresses weren't as sexy or thin and social networking wasn't 'what everyone does'. We had MySpace – but again, there was something inherently more innocent about it than what goes on today. A few moody pictures – 'I call this self–portrait, "Me"' – and a list of crap songs you liked. We didn't have fancy phones, and we weren't online 24/7.

Nowadays in the age of Facebook, we can all be 'celebrities', fawned on in cyberspace by our 'friends', uploading pictures of our supposedly thrilling lives – and who is going to be the most susceptible to this weird, empty, fake culture? Self-obsessed, insecure teenage girls.

Again, it's normal for teenage girls to be self-obsessed and insecure – but the combination of a globally public outlet to express it in, and an unforgiving society that demands they be thin (with massive arse and boobs, of course) and always look hot, fashionable and fuckable, but *also* tells them to remove the most potent signs of them actually *being* fuckable (body fat/body hair, which signals adulthood, sexual maturity) is, quite frankly, a fucking disaster.

These are child-adults posing as temptresses, suggesting sexual experience that belies their years. I worry for my sister, I worry for her friends. If you didn't know my sister, her Facebook profile could lead you to believe she was a stripper (sorry Little One, but that's the hard, cold truth).

So, after I saw her naked, childlike vagina, I knew I needed to act.

'Things go from worse to worse,' I muttered, 'I must save the bush!'

I went to her room. I sat down and explained to her that it is not normal to remove your pubic hair. We're meant to have pubic hair. I told her that it is an unfortunate aspect of porn that has penetrated mainstream consciousness and beauty rituals.

'Your vagina looks like a slab of plucked chicken,' I said, 'and when your pubes start to come back, you'll get spots on it. An acne-ridden slab of plucked chicken. Do you want to look like a porn-star with a spotty, slabby chicken vagina?'

'No.'

'There you go. And, if any boy you get it on with tells you you're weird for having pubes, tell him to switch off the hard-core stuff and hang out with real women. Also, tell him that you refuse to live your life through the gaze of male desires – desires and expectations that have been fucked up through pornography.'

'I don't understand.'

'You will.'

That is what feminism means to me. It means my little sister being able to be a proper woman. It means my little sister being able to be empowered by her brains and her wit, and not how she looks. It means my little sister being able to be a sexual being on her own terms – not pornography's. It means, put simply, saving the bush.

'You can tell whether some
misogynistic societal pressure is being exerted on
women by calmly enquiring, "And are men doing this,
as well?" If they aren't, chances are you're dealing
with what we strident feminists refer to as
"some total fucking bullshit".'

Caitlin Moran

ACKNOWLEDGEMENTS

We would like to thank all the women in this book who wrote their contributions with great verve and in record time so that we could put out this volume with its many voices during the month of March which celebrates women internationally. We are grateful to our graphic artists for making their remarkable talents available to readers. Many have donated their proceeds to charity. The team at Virago have been wonderful in their support: Lennie Goodings and our amazing editor Victoria Pepe have made the hard work and countless emails a pleasure.

Thank you all.

CONTRIBUTORS

Lisa Appignanesi OBE is a prize-winning writer, novelist and cultural commentator. She is Visiting Professor in Literature and Medical Humanities at King's College London, Chair of the Freud Museum, London, and outgoing President of English PEN. A former Deputy Director of London's Institute of Contemporary Arts, she has judged many literary prizes, has a PhD in comparative literature, and was made a Chevalier de l'Ordre des Arts et des Lettres in recognition of her contribution to literature. Her non-fiction includes *All About Love: Anatomy of an Unruly Emotion; Mad, Bad and Sad: A History of the Mind Doctors from 1800; Freud's Women* (with John Forrester); and a biography of Simone de Beauvoir. Her acclaimed family memoir, *Losing the Dead* comes out in a new edition from Virago this year. She has written nine novels, most recently *The Memory Man*. Lisa Appignanesi is currently working on *Dangerous to Know*, a book on the intersection of madness, the law and psychiatry in crimes of passion. She was awarded the OBE in January 2013.

Rachel Holmes is a writer, activist, historian and cultural programmer. Her next book *Eleanor Marx* is out shortly from Bloomsbury. She is the author of biographies of *The Secret Life of Dr James Barry* and *The Hottentot Venus: The Life and Death of Saartjie Baartman*. She was co-editor of *Sixty Six Books, 21st Century Writers Speak to the King James Bible*. Rachel was one of the launch team of Amazon.co.uk in 1998, and has since been director of the Southbank Centre Literature and Spoken Word programme, where she ran the London Literature Festival and Poetry International enabled by the inspirational leadership of feminist boss Jude Kelly.

She is a Writer in Residence at the PALFEST Palestine Writing Workshop in the occupied West Bank and Gaza and visiting lecturer at the Ndifuna Ukwazi Fellowship programme for active citizenship and leadership in South Africa. Rachel has judged various literature prizes, including the Orange Prize for Fiction. She sits on the boards of English PEN and Oxfam GB, and is a founder member of the feminist Oxfam Circle project. In 2010 Rachel received an Arts Council cultural leadership award as one of Britain's Fifty Women to Watch.

Susie Orbach is a psychoanalyst and writer who has been a feminist activist for decades. Her first book, *Fat is a Feminist Issue* (1978), was a key text for the Women's Liberation Movement and is still widely read and referred to. Other influential titles include *Hunger Strike*, *What Do Women Want?* (with Luise Eichenbaum), *The Impossibility of Sex* and her latest book, *Bodies*.

Susie co-founded the Women's Therapy Centre in London in 1976 and the Women's Therapy Centre Institute, New York in 1981. Her interests have centred around feminism and psychoanalysis, the construction of femininity and gender, globalization, body image, emotional literacy, and psychoanalysis and the public sphere.

She has been a consultant to the World Bank, the NHS and Unilever. She is a founder member of ANTIDOTE (working for emotional literacy) and Psychotherapists and Counsellors for Social Responsibility, and is convenor of Endangered Bodies (www.london.endangeredbodies.org) the organization campaigning against body hatred.

She is currently chair of the Relational School in the UK and has a clinical practice seeing individuals and couples.

Naomi Alderman is a novelist, games designer and writer. Her novels include *Disobedience*, which won the Orange Prize for New Writers and *The Liar's Gospel*. Her games include the top-selling smartphone game *Zombies, Run!*

Tahmima Anam was born in Dhaka, Bangladesh. Her first novel, *A Golden Age*, was shortlisted for the *Guardian* First Book Award and the Costa First Novel Prize, and was the Winner of the 2008 Commonwealth Writers' Prize for Best First Book. Her second novel, *The Good Muslim* was published in 2011 and is shortlisted for the 2013 DSC Prize for South Asian literature, confirming 'Anam as one of our most important novelists' (*Sunday Telegraph*). She lives in London.

Margaret Atwood is the author of more than forty works, including fiction, poetry and critical essays, and her books have been published in over thirty-five countries. Of her novels, *The Blind Assassin* won the 2000 Booker Prize and *Alias Grace* won the Giller Prize in Canada and the Premio Mondello in Italy. *The Year of the Flood* (2009) is Margaret Atwood's most recent novel. In 2005 she was the recipient of the Edinburgh Book Festival Enlightenment Award, for a distinguished contribution to world literature and thought. In 2008, Margaret Atwood was awarded the Prince of Asturias Prize for Literature in Spain. She lives in Toronto.

Joan Bakewell has been a leading broadcaster and journalist for four decades. She has published seven books, including two novels, *All the Nice Girls* and *She's Leaving Home*. As Baroness Bakewell, she is a Labour Peer in the House of Lords and between 2008 and 2010, acted as a voice of older people'.

Camila Batmanghelidjh is the founder of two children's charities – Place2Be (now national) and Kids Company, where she currently works with some of the most traumatized young people living in London. She trained as a psychotherapist, engaged in twenty years of psychoanalysis and has become an advocate for vulnerable children. In 2009 she was named Business Woman of the Year for the Dods and Scottish Widows Public Life Awards. She won the lifetime achievement award from the Centre of Social Justice. Kids Company has been awarded the Human Rights Awards by Liberty and JUSTICE and has been awarded Child Poverty Champion Status by the End Child Poverty Action Group.

Alison Bechdel is acclaimed for her pioneering strip *Dykes to Watch Out For*, which first appeared in 1986 and now has an international following. She is also the author–illustrator of two innovative graphic memoirs, *Fun Home: A Family Tragicomic* and *Are You My Mother?: A Comic Drama*.

Bidisha is a writer, critic and TV and radio broadcaster specializing in the arts and culture, social justice and international affairs. She is a regular commentator on the radio and television and has judged the Orange Prize and the John Llewellyn Rhys prize, among others. She also writes for a wide range of publications. She is the author of two novels as well as the bestselling travel memoir *Venetian Masters: Under the Skin of the City of Love* and the internationally acclaimed reportage *Beyond the Wall: Writing a Path Through Palestine*. She is currently working on her fifth book, about asylum seekers and refugees.

Lydia Cacho is a Mexican journalist and feminist activist. Author of seven books, including *Slavery Inc: The Untold Story of International Sex Trafficking* (Portobello), she is the winner of the UNESCO World Press Freedom Prize, the Tucholsky Award and the PEN Pinter Prize 2010, amongst others. She publishes a weekly column in twenty newspapers in Mexico. She is the first woman in Mexican history to have taken to court an organized child pornography and woman-trafficking crime ring. This has resulted in many threats on her life.

Shami Chakrabarti has been Director of Liberty (the National Council for Civil Liberties) since September 2003. Shami first joined Liberty as In-House Counsel on 10 September 2001. She became heavily involved in its engagement with the 'War on Terror' and with the defence and promotion of human rights values in Parliament, the Courts and wider society. Since becoming Liberty's Director she has written, spoken and broadcast widely on the importance of the post-Second World War human rights framework as an essential component of democratic society. She was recently invited to be one of six independent assessors advising Lord Justice Leveson in his Public Inquiry into the Culture, Practice and Ethics of the UK Press.

Jane Czyzselska is the editor of *DIVA* magazine, Britain's leading monthly for gay and bisexual women. She writes for a range of publications including the *Independent on Sunday*, the *Guardian* and *The Times* and is a regular host and panellist at LGBT debates and events. She is a trustee of the LGBT mental-health charity PACE and is studying for a master's degree in psychotherapy.

Sayantani DasGupta is a physician and writer whose scholarly work is in the field of feminist health science studies. She is a widely published and nationally recognized speaker on issues of narrative, health care, race, gender, and medical education. She is the co-author of *The Demon Slayers and Other Stories: Bengali Folk Tales*, the author of a memoir, *Her Own Medicine*, about her education at Johns Hopkins University, and the co-editor of an award-winning collection of women's illness narratives, *Stories of Illness and Healing: Women Write Their Bodies*.

Not only author and illustrator of *Mistakes In The Background*, *Ugly Shy Girl* and *Echoes*, **Laura Dockrill** also resurrects her words on the stage, performing poetry spanning festivals to bookshops. Named one of the top ten literary talents by *The Times* and one of the top twenty hot faces to watch by *ELLE* magazine, Laura continues to stir up the literary universe with her passionate, contemporary and imaginative way with words. Laura Dockrill is currently creating a series of bespoke artwork pieces and writing both a piece of work for a new BBC radio show and a sitcom. Random House Children's division recently published the first in a new 'tween' series of books.

Lynne Featherstone served on the London Assembly from 2000–5, before being elected as Liberal Democrat MP for Hornsey and Wood Green. In December 2007, after Nick Clegg's election as party leader, she switched to the role of Youth and Equalities Spokesperson in the Shadow Cabinet. During this time, Lynne Featherstone introduced proposals for Equal Marriage and the first Transgender Action Plan in the world. In her Home Office portfolio she looked after domestic violence and was also appointed as Ministerial Champion for tackling Violence against Women and girls across the world.

Carlene Firmin MBE, Principal Policy Advisor at the Office of the Children's Commissioner, is Advisor and Head of the Secretariat for the CSEGG (Child Sexual Exploitation in Gangs and Groups) Inquiry, and is currently undertaking a professional doctorate at the University of Bedfordshire looking at the concept of 'peer-on-peer' abuse in young people's relationships. Carlene authored the two Female Voice in Violence reports which led to national and local government change in dealing with the impact of gang violence on women and girls. Carlene writes a monthly column in *Society Guardian*, and has had a number of papers published in academic books and journals.

Lennie Goodings is the Publisher of Virago Press.

Linda Grant is a novelist and journalist. She won the Orange Prize for Fiction in 2000 and the Lettre Ulysses Prize for Literary Reportage in 2006, and was shortlisted for the Man Booker in 2008 for *The Clothes on Their Backs*.

Nathalie Handal is the author of numerous books, most recently *Poet in Andalucía,* which Alice Walker lauds as 'poems of depth and weight and the sorrowing song of longing and resolve'; *Love and Strange Horses,* winner of the 2011 Gold Medal Independent Publisher Book Award, which the *New York Times* says is 'a book that trembles with belonging (and longing)'; and the landmark anthology *Language for a New Century: Contemporary Poetry from the Middle East, Asia & Beyond*. She is a Lannan Foundation Fellow, winner of the Alejo Zuloaga Order in Literature 2011, among other honours.

*

Natalie Haynes is a regular panellist on BBC2's *The Review Show,* and appeared on *Newsnight Review* for its final three years. She has appeared as a panellist on BBC 4's *The Book Quiz,* and on *Poetry Special* alongside Andrew Motion and George Szirtes. She has also spoken about 3D film for Channel 4, and the scifi series *Flashforward* for Channel 5. She was also a panellist on the geekiest quiz of the modern era – *Mindgames,* with Simon Singh – and featured in a Liberty Bell series about school reports, *Must Try Harder,* screened on BBC2 in 2006. She can occasionally be seen on the news, banging on about Harry Potter (good) and ID cards (bad). In 2012 Natalie Haynes was an Orange Prize judge.

Sharon Haywood, a Canadian freelance writer and editor living in Buenos Aires, is part of the international movement Endangered Bodies, a local–global initiative challenging the merchants of body hatred. She acts as a virtual member of the

AnyBody/Endangered Bodies UK team and is the founder of the Buenos Aires chapter, AnyBody Argentina. Additionally, Sharon is co-editor for AdiosBarbie.com, a website devoted to promoting healthy body image and identity in folks of all races, sizes, sexual orientations and identities, abilities and ages. Her writing, both in English and Spanish, can be found in print and online in outlets such as Canada's leading feminist magazine *Herizons* and national Argentine newspapers.

Lindsey Hilsum is Channel 4 News' International Editor and the author of *Sandstorm; Libya in the Time of Revolution* (Faber, 2012). She has covered the wars in Iraq, Afghanistan and Kosovo, the Israeli-Palestinian conflict and the genocide in Rwanda. In 2011 she reported the Arab Spring uprisings in Libya and Egypt. From 2006–8 she was based in China. She has been Royal Television Society Journalist of the Year, and won awards from Amnesty International and One World Media, as well as the Charles Wheeler and James Cameron awards. She contributes to the *Sunday Times*, the *Observer* and *Granta*.

Isabel Hilton is a London-based writer and broadcaster with a career that spans print, electronic and online media in the UK and internationally. She has reported extensively from East and South Asia, Latin America, Europe and Africa, and her work has been published in many of the world's major media. In addition to her writing career, she is a radio presenter and has presented several documentaries on radio and television. She holds honorary doctorates from the universities of Bradford and Stirling and was appointed OBE in recognition of her work in raising environmental awareness in China.

Siri Hustvedt is the author of five novels, *The Blindfold, The Enchantment of Lily Dahl, What I Loved, The Sorrows of an American* and *The Summer Without Men*; three collections of essays, *A Plea for Eros*, *Mysteries of the Rectangle*, and *Living, Thinking, Looking*, as well as the non-fiction work, *The Shaking Woman or A History of My Nerves*. Her work has been translated into over thirty languages. She is the 2012 recipient of the International Gabarron Award for Thought and Humanities. She lives in Brooklyn, New York.

Jude Kelly is the Artistic Director of Southbank Centre, Britain's largest cultural institution. She founded Solent People's Theatre and Battersea Arts Centre, and was the Artistic Director of the York Festival and Mystery Plays. In 1997 she was awarded the OBE for her services to the theatre. She has directed over a hundred productions, including the Royal Shakespeare Company, the National Theatre and the Théâtre du Châtelet in Paris and in the West End. Jude Kelly is Chair of the Trustees for World Book Night, and sits on the Cultural Olympiad Board, which was responsible for the ongoing framework for delivering the creative, cultural and educational aspects of London's Olympic and Paralympic Games in 2012.

Liz Kelly was founder of the Refuge Women's Centre and Rape Crisis Centre when living in Norwich. For the last thirty years she has undertaken independent research on violence against women and she heads up the Child and Woman Abuse Studies Unit at the London Metropolitan University. She is co-Chair of the unique and influential feminist coalition End Violence Against Women (EVAW).

Helena Kennedy is a barrister, broadcaster and Labour member of the House of Lords. She is an expert in human rights law, civil liberties and constitutional issues and is the Chair of Justice – the British arm of the International Commission of Jurists. She recently led an Inquiry for the Equality and Human Rights Commission on

Human Trafficking in Scotland and is currently a member of the Government Commission on a British Bill of Rights.

Kathy Lette first achieved *success de scandale* as a teenager with the novel *Puberty Blues*, which was made into a major film and a TV mini-series. After several years as a newspaper columnist and television sitcom writer in Los Angeles and New York, she wrote twelve international bestsellers, including *Mad Cows* (the film starred Joanna Lumley and Anna Friel), *How to Kill Your Husband and Other Handy Household Hints*, *To Love, Honour and Betray* and *The Boy Who Fell To Earth*. She is an ambassador for Women and Children First, Plan International and the White Ribbon Alliance. Kathy is an autodidact (a word she taught herself) but in 2010 received an honorary doctorate from Southampton Solent University.

Kate Mosse is a novelist, non-fiction writer and playwright. Her number-one international bestselling Languedoc Trilogy – *Labyrinth, Sepulchre* and *Citadel* – and her novella, *The Winter Ghosts*, have sold millions of copies throughout the world. *Labyrinth* was named as one of the Top Twenty-Five novels of the past twenty-five years and has been filmed as a mini-series by Ridley and Tony Scott's Scott Free for Channel 4. A campaigner for the library service and for literacy, Kate is Co-founder and Chair of the Women's Prize for Fiction (previously the Orange Prize for Fiction), which comes of age in 2013.

Laurie Penny is an author, journalist and activist from London. She is twenty-six years old and is Contributing Editor at the *New Statesman*. She doesn't usually write poetry.

Lisa Power is the Director of Policy for Terrence Higgins Trust, the UK's largest sexual health and HIV charity. She has spent most of her life active in LGBT and sexual-health issues, from

London Gay Switchboard to the International Lesbian & Gay Association via Stonewall, the *Pink Paper*, ActUp and the short lived but enjoyable DAFT (Dykes and Faggots Together). She founded the first lesbian sex-toy mail-order business in the UK, Thrilling Bits, and she was the first openly LGBT person to speak on lesbian and gay rights at the United Nations.

Nina Power is a Senior Lecturer in Philosophy at Roehampton University and a Tutor in Critical Writing in Art and Design at the Royal College of Art. She has written widely on European philosophy, feminism and politics.

Pussy Riot are a Russian feminist punk collective. On 21 February 2012 they staged a performance in the Cathedral of Christ the Saviour in Moscow. Three of their members were later arrested and charged with felony hooliganism motivated by religious hatred. Their arrest provoked international protest.

Alissa Quart is the author of three works of literary non-fiction, *Branded: The Buying and Selling of Teenagers*, *Hothouse Kids*, and the forthcoming *Republic of Outsiders*. She has written for many newspapers and magazines on feminism and youth, including the *New York Times* and the *Atlantic*. She writes a feminist column for *New York Magazine* called Broadside and one for the *Columbia Journalism Review* on documentary culture. Alissa is also editor-at-large of the *Atavist* and an adjunct professor at Columbia University's Graduate School of Journalism. She was a 2010 Nieman Fellow at Harvard. Her poetry has been published in the *London Review of Books*, *Feminist Studies*, and the *Awl*, among other publications.

Diana Quick has worked as an actress since her debut in a BBC Wednesday Play in 1964. She translated and performed in Simone de Beauvoir's *The Woman Destroyed*, published by

Methuen. Her family memoir, *A Tug on the Thread* is published by Virago. She has been director of the annual Aldeburgh Documentary Festival for the last three years. She was the first female president of the Oxford University Dramatic Society in 1968, the year of the half-centenary of universal Women's Suffrage in the UK.

Josie Rourke was born in Salford, Greater Manchester. She read English at Cambridge University and trained as the Resident Assistant Director at the Donmar Warehouse, was Trainee Associate Director at the Royal Court Theatre, Associate Director at Sheffield Theatres and Artistic Director of the Bush Theatre which, in 2011, she moved into its new home. Josie is Artistic Director of London's Donmar Warehouse and is a Board Member of Channel 4 and a Fellow of the Royal Society of Arts.

Bee Rowlatt is a BBC World Service journalist and co-author of *Talking About Jane Austen in Baghdad*. She has written for the *Telegraph*, the *Independent*, *The Times*, and *Grazia*. Public speaking appearances include the Oxford Literary Festival, Hay Festival, and British Council events in Iraq, Norway and Palestine. She won the Society of Authors' K. Blundell Trust award to complete the travels in her current book, which is inspired by the life of Mary Wollstonecraft. Bee has four children and lives in London.

Elif Shafak is an award-winning novelist and the most widely read woman writer in Turkey. Her books have been translated into more than thirty languages and she was awarded the honorary distinction of Chevalier de l'Ordre des Arts et des Lettres. Elif Shafak has published twelve books, including eight novels. Her novels include *The Bastard of Istanbul*, *The Forty Rules of Love*, and *The Honour*, which was published in April 2012 by Penguin. She has a column in a major Turkish newspaper and contributes to newspapers and magazines around the world, including the *New York Times*, the *Guardian* and *Corriere della Sera*.

Hanan Al-Shaykh was born in Lebanon and grew up in Beirut. She was educated in Cairo and wrote her first novel there when she was nineteen before returning to Beirut to work as a journalist for *Al-Nahar*'s newspaper *Al Hasna Magazine*. In 1975 she left Beirut because of the civil war, and since 1984 she has lived in London. Her work has been translated into twenty-five languages and is published around the world. Six of her novels have been translated into English – her novel *Only in London* was shortlisted for the *Independent* Foreign Fiction Prize.

Muneeza Shamsie is a Pakistani journalist and critic. She is bibliographer (Pakistan) for the *Journal of Commonwealth Literature,* guest editor of *The Journal of Postcolonial Writing 47.2* (Pakistan issue) and editor of three pioneering anthologies including *And The World Changed: Contemporary Stories by Pakistani Women* which won the 2009 IPPY (Gold) and the 2008 Foreword (Bronze) Awards in the United States. She is a judge for the 2013 DSC Prize for South Asian literature and from 2009–11 served as regional chair (Eurasia) for the Commonwealth Writers Prize. She lives in Karachi. Muneeza Shamsie is Kamila Shamsie's mother and Attia Hosain's niece.

Elaine Showalter is Professor Emeritus of English and Avalon Professor of the Humanities at Princeton University. She has written ten books, most recently the literary history *A Jury of Her Peers: American Women Writers from Anne Bradstreet to Annie Proulx* (Virago, 2009), which was awarded the Truman Capote Prize for Literary Criticism. Showalter has served as President of the Modern Language Association, and has been awarded fellowships by the Guggenheim Foundation, Mellon Foundation, and the Rockefeller Foundation. Showalter has been a judge for the National Book Awards (US), the National Magazine Fiction

Awards (US), and the Orange Prize for Fiction (UK), and chaired the Man Booker International Fiction Prize.

Posy Simmonds is a cartoonist, illustrator and author based in London.

Gillian Slovo is the author of twelve novels, including *Red Dust*, which was made into a film starring Hilary Swank and Chiwetel Ejiofor; *Ice Road*, which was shortlisted for the 2004 Orange Price for Fiction; and, most recently, *An Honourable Man*. Her family memoir, *Every Secret Thing*, was an international bestseller. Her play *Guantanamo*, co-written for the Tricycle Theatre, has played in theatres around the world, including in New York and Washington DC. She is the President of English PEN.

Ahdaf Soueif, a citizen of Egypt and the UK, is the author of the bestselling *The Map of Love* (shortlisted for the Booker Prize in 1999 and translated into thirty languages), as well as the well-loved *In the Eye of the Sun* and the collection of short stories, *I Think of You*. Ahdaf Soueif is also a political and cultural commentator. In 2007 Ahdaf Soueif founded Engaged Events, a UK-based charity. Its first project is the Palestine Festival of Literature, which takes place in the occupied cities of Palestine and in Gaza. Ahdaf Soueif's account of Egyptian events, *Cairo: my City, our Revolution*, was published by Bloomsbury in January 2012.

Martha Spurrier is a barrister who specialises in mental health, public law and human rights. She has a particular interest in women's rights and access to justice. When she is not lawyering, Martha enjoys food, talking to women and watching plays.

Juliet Stevenson is one of Britain's leading actors. She has worked extensively for the Royal Shakespeare Company, the National Theatre and the Royal Court, winning an Oliver for her performance as Pauline in *Death and the Maiden* in 1991. Her films include *Truly, Madly Deeply*, *Bend it Like Beckham*, *When Did You Last See Your Father?*, *Being Julia*, *Pierrepoint*, *Mona Lisa Smile* and *Caught in Flight*. Recent television work includes *Place of Execution*, *The Hour* and *White Heat*. She is currently filming a new series for the BBC, *The Village*. She was awarded the CBE in 1999.

Alice Stride was born in 1988. She is one of five children (three boys and two girls), the result of which is a) being a staunch feminist and b) talking too loudly. She has a degree in English Literature and is utterly thrilled to be a part of *Fifty Shades of Feminism*.

Meera Syal is a writer and performer best known for her work on the award-winning *Goodness Gracious Me*, the film *Bhaji on the Beach* and the musical *Bombay Dreams*. Recently, as a writer, she has developed and written the first episode of an original three-part series *Heal Me* for Touchpaper/BBC, written a play for the National Theatre's Connections 2012 season and started work on her third novel for Transworld.

Born and brought up in east London to Jamaican parents, **Shirley J. Thompson** has gained a reputation for her masterful synthesis of original contemporary classical orchestral music with a range of popular styles to produce a distinct voice in twenty-first-century composition. Thompson's pioneering vision in devising concepts and narratives that underpin her work has led to her creating highly imaginative productions. A cutting-edge composer, her music is performed, screened and broadcast worldwide: Thompson is the first woman in Europe to have composed and conducted a symphony within the last forty years.

After graduating from Cambridge, **Sandi Toksvig** went into theatre as a writer and performer. Well known for her television and radio work as a presenter, writer and actor, she has written more than twenty books for children and adults. Her most recent novel is *Valentine Grey* (Virago, 2012). She also writes for theatre and television: her film *The Man*, starring Stephen Fry and Zoë Wanamaker, was broadcast on Sky Arts in June 2012 and her play *Bully Boy*, starring Anthony Andrews, opened the St James Theatre, London, autumn 2012. She is the new Chancellor of Portsmouth University. Sandi Toksvig lives in London and Kent.

Natasha Walter is author of *The New Feminism* and, most recently, *Living Dolls* (Virago, 2010). She is a journalist and broadcaster, and the director of Women for Refugee Women.

Marilyn Waring is Professor of Public Policy at AUT University in New Zealand where she supervises research degrees. She is author of the classic *Counting for Nothing/ If Women Counted* and is a development consultant and human rights and environmental activist.

Timberlake Wertenbaker is a playwright, whose plays include *Our Country's Good*, *The Grace of Mary Traverse* and *Three Birds Alighting on a Field* (Royal Court). Among her other works are *The Love of the Nightingale* (RSC), *Galileo's Daughter* (Theatre Royal, Bath), and *The Line* (Arcola Theatre). She is currently writing a new play for Out of Joint.

Timberlake was the Leverhulme Artist in Residence at the Freud Museum in 2011 and is currently the UNESCO City of Literature Visiting Professor of Creative Writing at the University of East Anglia.

Jeanette Winterson OBE writes fiction, essays, screenplays and journalism. Her most recent work, *Why Be Happy When You Could Be Normal?*, is a worldwide bestseller.

Xuē Xīnrán (薛欣然, pen name *Xinran*) is a British-Chinese journalist and broadcaster, born in Beijing in 1958. In 1997 she
moved to London, where she initially worked as cleaner. She
began work on her seminal book about Chinese women's lives
The Good Women of China, a memoir relating many of the stories
she heard while hosting her radio show in China. The book was
published in 2002 and has been translated into over thirty languages. She has written a further five books, including *Sky Burial*,
What the Chinese Don't Eat and, most recently, *Message from an
Unknown Chinese Mother*, a collection of heartbreaking stories
from Chinese mothers who have lost or had to abandon children.
Xīnrán advises the BBC and Sky about western relations with
China and was the founder, in 2004, of The Mother's Bridge of
Love, a charity helping Chinese children across the world.

COPYRIGHT ACKNOWLEDGEMENTS